QUICK STATS

Basics for Medical Literature Evaluation

FIFTH EDITION

Charles Herring

Editors:
Asima Ali
Patience Thompson

Printed in the United States of America

ISBN 13: 978-1-58390-207-3

Cover Image: © Can Stock Photo Inc./

530 Great Road
Acton, MA 01720
800-562-2147

I want to acknowledge those, without whom, I would be as completely lost as I was many years ago when I first started learning how to evaluate medical literature: Dan Neal, PharmD, BCPS, Karen Neal, PharmD, BCPS, G. Robert DeYoung, PharmD, BCPS, Janet Pitner, PharmD, BCPS, Richard Drew, PharmD, MS, BCPS, Antoine Al-Achi, PhD, Gary Dunham, PharmD, BCPS, Keith S. Kaye, MD, MPH, Nanette Berensen, PharmD, BCPS, Melanie Pound, PharmD, BCPS, Connie Barnes, PharmD, Kathey Fulton Rumley, PharmD, Brenda Jamerson, PharmD, and Mary Townsend, PharmD, AAHIVP.

I want to thank my colleagues and the staff at Campbell University and the Downtown Health Plaza of Wake Forest University Baptist Medical Center, and our residents and students who have helped make composing and dispersing this work possible. I especially want to recognize that Campbell University Doctor of Pharmacy Class of 2015 for their contributions to this edition.

Most of all, I want to thank God for everything, especially for my supportive family and friends. I love you. You are the greatest!

Charles Herring, PharmD, BCPS, CPP

This book is most helpful when used in combination with a series of works by Drs. Gaddis & Gaddis, published in the 1990 *Annals of Emergency Medicine*.[1-6]

Table of Contents **Pages**

Abbreviations	
# = number μ = population mean α = alpha β = beta Δ = delta ACEI = angiotensin converting enzyme inhibitor ADR = adverse drug reaction Afib = atrial fibrillation AE = adverse effect aka = also known as ALLHAT = see Reference #22 ANBP2 = see Reference #23 ANACOVA = analysis of covariance ANCOVA = analysis of covariance ANOVA = analysis of variance AR_C = absolute risk of the control group AR_E = absolute risk of the experimental group ARB = angiotensin receptor blocker ARF = acute renal failure ARI = absolute risk increase ARR = absolute risk reduction ASCVD = atherosclerotic cardiovascular disease b/c = because b/n = between BP = blood pressure BUN = blood urea nitrogen CA = cancer CE = composite or combined endpoint CER = control group event rate CI = confidence interval COPD = chronic obstructive pulmonary disease COX-2 = cyclooxygenase 2 CV = cardiovascular DES = diethylstilbestrol diff = difference DM = diabetes mellitus DVT = deep vein thrombosis dysfx = dysfunction ED = emergency department EER = experimental group event rate	EF = ejection fraction endpts = endpoints ERT = estrogen replacement therapy FEV_1 = forced expiratory volume in 1 second FN = false negative FP = false positive GI = gastrointestinal H_o = null hypothesis H_1 = alternative hypothesis HCTZ = hydrochlorothiazide HDL = high density lipoprotein HF = heart failure HIV = human immunodeficiency virus HR = hazard ratio; heart rate HTN = hypertension IBW = ideal body weight IRB = institutional review board ITT = intention-to-treat analysis IV = intravenous LDL = low density lipoprotein LIFE = see Reference # 24 LOCF = last observation carried forward LV = left ventricular MA = meta-analysis Meds = medications MI = myocardial infarction mITT = modified intention-to-treat mmHg = millimeters of mercury MRA = multiple or multivariate regression analysis MRI = magnetic resonance imaging N or n = number of patients NI = non-inferior or non-inferiority NNH = number needed to harm NNT = number needed to treat NPV = negative predictive value NSAID = non-steroidal anti-inflammatory drug NSS = not statistically significant or non-statistically significant NYHA = new york heart association OC = oral contraceptive

Abbreviations continued
OR = odds ratio PPV = positive predictive value PSM = propensity score matching pt = patient pts = patients PVD = peripheral vascular disease RCT = randomized controlled trial RR = relative risk RRI = relative risk increase RRR = relative risk reduction SA = subgroup analysis SCr = serum creatinine SD = standard deviation SEM = standard error of the mean SS = statistically significant TC = total cholesterol TN = true negative TP = true positive txment = treatment ValHeFT = see Reference # 25 Vs = versus w/ = with yrs = years $\bar{X}$ = mean or average

Part 1: Basic Concepts[1]

Sample vs Population:

- It is impossible to survey all individuals in a population. Only a subset of a population is practical to evaluate due to cost and time considerations. If a representative sample of an appropriate population can be obtained and studied, conclusions regarding the sample may be extrapolated to the defined population.

Variables:

A **Random Variable** is "a **variable whose** observed **values may be considered as outcomes of an experiment** and whose values **cannot be anticipated with certainty before the experiment is conducted"**[8]

- Discrete variables (aka as counting or non-parametric)[7,8]
- Continuous variables (aka measuring or parametric)[7,8]

"**Independent Variable**: the intervention or what is being manipulated" in a study. (aka the intervention of the study; e.g. a drug being evaluated).[15] "Independent variables define the conditions under which the dependent variable is to be examined. There may be zero, one, or many independent variables. The number of independent variables determines the category of statistical methods that are appropriate to use."[15]

"**Dependent Variable**: the outcome of interest within a study"[15] [aka endpoint of the study; e.g., hospitalization, death, blood pressure (BP), cholesterol]. It is "the outcome that one intends to explain or estimate."[15] There may be multiple dependent variables.

- Example: A trial is evaluating chlorthalidone's effect on hospitalization. The independent variable is chlorthalidone. The dependent variable is hospitalization.

Analyses: Univariable, Bivariable, and Multivariable

Univariable Analysis: there is "one dependent variable and no independent variables."[15] For example, estimating the annual risk for cardiovascular death (dependent variable) in a community without regard to any characteristics like smoking status, age, sex, hypertension, diabetes, etc.[15]

Bivariable Analysis: there is "one dependent variable and one independent variable."[15] For example, estimating the annual risk for cardiovascular death (dependent variable) in a community with regard to one characteristic (or independent variable) like smoking status.[15]

Multivariable Analysis: there is one dependent variable and ≥ 2 independent variables." For example, estimating the annual risk for cardiovascular death (dependent variable) in a community with regard to at least 2 characteristics (or independent variables). (e.g., smoking status, age, sex, and ethnicity).[15]
NOTE: "Multivariable methods are frequently used to adjust for the influence of confounding variables" as is discussed later.[15]

Types of Data

Non-parametric (aka Discrete) Variables

- **Nominal**: Numbers are purely arbitrary or without regard to any order of ranking of severity.[1,7,8,11,12] Nominal data may be dichotomous or categorical.
    - Dichotomous (binary): lived/died, yes/no, hospitalized/not hospitalized.[11,12]
    - Categorical: There is no order or inherent value for nominal, categorical data. [e.g., race, eye color, hair color, religion, blood type, acute renal failure (ARF)/heart failure (HF)/diabetes mellitus (DM)][11,12]
- **Ordinal**: Categorical, but scored on a continuum, *without* a consistent level of magnitude of difference between ranks[1,7,8,11,12] (e.g., pain scale, NYHA class, trauma score, Glasgow coma score, Likert-like scales-poor/fair/good/very good/excellent, cancer staging, bruise staging, military rank).[1,8,11,12,15,27]
    - Since ordinal data are non-parametric or non-normally distributed and there is a lack of any consistent magnitude of difference between units, the central tendency estimate of mean (aka average) is usually misleading.[1,15] Median and mode may be used as measures of central tendency for ordinal data.
    - Since ordinal data are non-parametric or non-normally distributed, standard deviation (SD) as a measure of variability is generally avoided for ordinal data. An interquartile range is the choice measure of variability for ordinal data.

Parametric (aka Continuous or Measuring) Variables: These are on a continuum with a consistent level of magnitude of difference between data units. Although the specific definitions of the two types of parametric data are listed below, their definitions are somewhat academic since all parametric data utilizes the same statistical tests. In other words, regardless of whether the parametric data are interval or ratio scale, the same tests are used to detect statistical differences.

- Both interval and ratio scale parametric data have a predetermined order to their numbering and a consistent level of magnitude of difference between the observed data units.[1,7,8,11,12] However, for interval scale data, there is no absolute zero.[1,7,8]

(e.g., Celsius or Fahrenheit)[1,8] There is an absolute zero for ratio scale data.[1,7,8] (e.g., drug concentrations, plasma glucose, FEV_1, Kelvin, heart rate, BP, # of platelets, distance, time)[1,7,8,12]

- Although it is not likely you will see this in practice, parametric data can be degraded to ordinal data or nominal data.[1] However, it is impossible to upgrade data. It is impossible to upgrade nominal data to ordinal data and it is impossible to upgrade ordinal data to parametric data.[1] For example, we can degrade parametric data (blood pressures) to ordinal data (hypertension stages: prehypertension, stage 1, and stage 2). We can further degrade the data to nominal (non-hypertensive vs hypertensive). It should be clear from this example that it is impossible to upgrade nominal data (non-hypertensive vs hypertensive) to ordinal data (hypertension stages) or to parametric data (blood pressures).

Distributions[1]

- **Normal distribution**: aka bell-shaped curve, Gaussian curve, curve of error, or normal probability curve.[11,15]

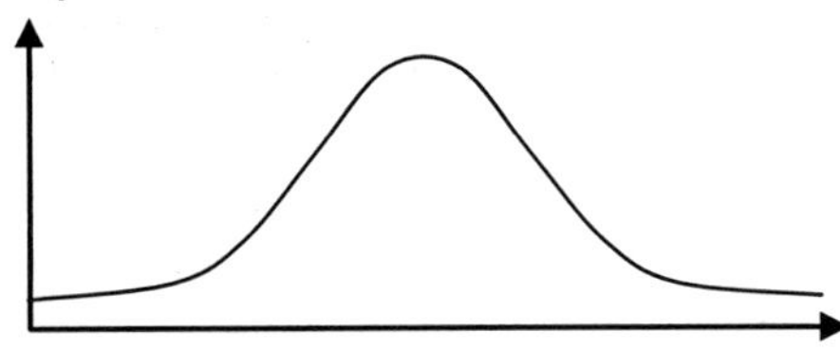

- **Bimodal distribution**: 2 peaks of cluster, or areas of high frequency. (average male vs female weight)[1,7]

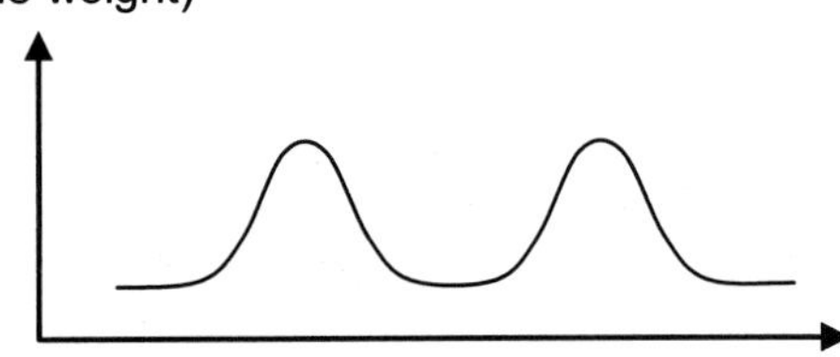

- **Rectangular distribution**: frequency of date of birth (month and day)[1]

- **Skewed distribution**: data tail off to either the high or low end of measurement units.[1,7]

  - **Positive skew**: cluster of data on the low end. [e.g., the X axis could be the income of patients seen in inner-city emergency department (ED), cost of generic medications, number of prescribed medications in patients younger than 30 years (yrs) of age][1,7]

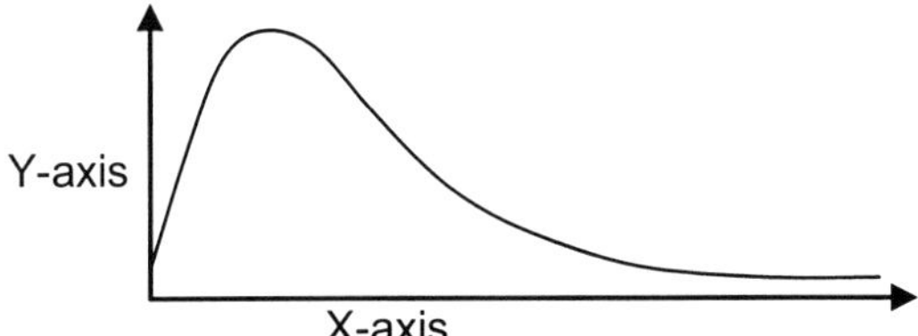

  - **Negative skew**: cluster of data on the high end. (e.g., the X axis could be the income of patients seen in ED of an affluent area, cost of brand name medications, number of prescribed medications in patients older than 60 yrs of age)[1,7]

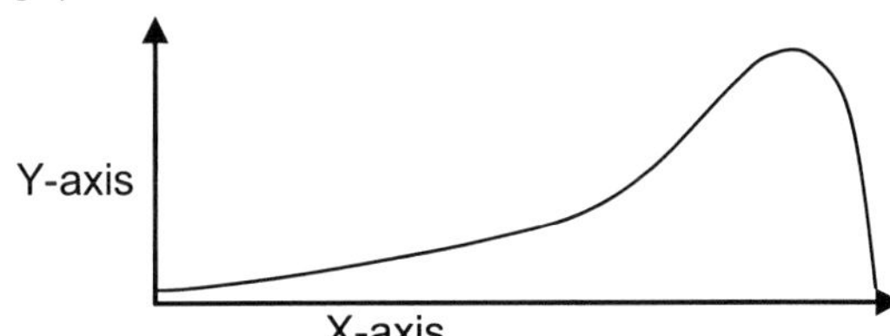

- **Kurtosis**: when each end of the graph tails up and clusters on both ends of the graph (e.g., the J-curve of hypertension treatment; with the J-curve, mortality increases if blood pressure is either too high or too low.)[7,11]

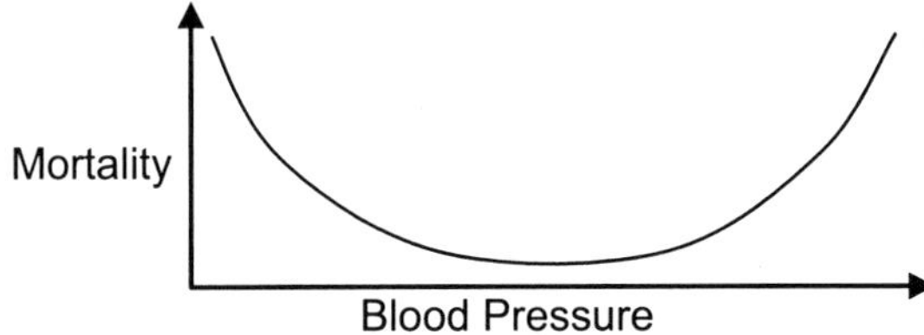

Study Questions: (provided by Melanie Pound, PharmD, BCPS)

1. What are some examples of parametric data?

2. A researcher wishes to assess the number of patients who are receiving vancomycin in a local hospital. Which type of analysis would be used to analyze the data?
   a. Univariable because there is one dependent and no independent variables
   b. Bivariable because there is one dependent and one independent variable
   c. Multivariable because there is one dependent and more than one independent variable
   d. Either bivariable or multivariable would be appropriate in this study

3. A researcher is planning to study the effects of caffeine on test performance among pharmacy students. The students will be analyzed according to age, gender, and use of psychiatric medications. Which of the following types of analysis would be BEST to utilize in analyzing the data?
   a. Univariable because there is one dependent and no independent variables.
   b. Bivariable because there is one dependent and one independent variable.
   c. Multivariable because there is one dependent and multiple independent variables.
   d. Multivariable because there are multiple dependent and multiple independent variables.

4. A researcher wishes to study the association of fetal cleft palate defects related to maternal folate deficiency during pregnancy. Which type of analysis would be used to analyze the data?
   a. Univariable because there is one dependent and no independent variable
   b. Univariable because there is one dependent and one independent variable
   c. Bivariable because there is one dependent and one independent variable
   d. Multivariable because there is one independent variable and multiple dependent variables

5. Which of the following BEST describes nonparametric data?
   a. Blood pressure, race, disease state, gender, age > 40
   b. Heart rate, temperature, NYHA class, pain scale, gender
   c. Ejection fraction, BMI, drug concentration, temperature, blood pressure
   d. Race, Sex, Mortality, hospitalization due to cardiovascular causes, NYHA class

Answers to Study Questions:

1. Body mass index (BMI), drug concentration, blood pressure, glucose, glycosylated hemoglobin (A1c).

2. a - The dependent variable is the number of patients who are receiving vancomycin.

3. c - The dependent variable is test performance. The independent variables include caffeine intake, age, gender, and use of psychiatric medications.

4. c - The dependent variable is fetal cleft palate defects. The independent variable is maternal folate deficiency during pregnancy.

5. d - Non-parametric data include nominal and ordinal data. Race, disease state, gender, age>40, sex, mortality, and hospitalization due to cardiovascular causes are nominal since there is no ranking or order. NYHA class and pain scale are ordinal since they are scored on a continuum, but there is no consistent level of magnitude of difference between the data points. Blood pressure, heart rate, temperature, ejection fraction, body mass index (BMI), and drug concentration are parametric since they are scored on a continuum and there is a consistent level of magnitude of difference between data points.

Part 2: Descriptive Statistics[2]

Measures of Central Tendency

- **Mean** (aka average): "sum of all values divided by the total number of values."[8] Mean is used for parametric (interval or ratio) data.[2,8] The mean is affected by outliers (extreme values).[2,8,11,15] Mu (μ) is the population mean. [8,15] X-bar ($\bar{X}$) is the sample mean.[2,8,15]

- **Median** (aka 50th percentile)[15]: the "mid-most" point.[2,11] The median is "the point above which or below which half of the data points lie." [15] It is not affected by outliers.[2,8,15] Median is used when outliers exist, data set spans a wide range of values, or "when continuous data are not normally distributed."[2,11,15,27] It may be used for ordinal or continuous (interval or ratio) data.[2,8,15]

    - Outcome frequency for ordinal data is also measured using proportions (1/4, 1/3, 1/2) or percentiles (25%, 33%, 50%), or median or mode.[11]

- **Mode**: the most common value.[2,8,15] It is useful for bimodal distributions.[2] It may be used for nominal, ordinal, or parametric (interval or ratio) data.[2,8,15] As with median, the mode is not affected by outliers.[2] However, the mode is not helpful when a data set contains a large range of infrequently occurring values.[2,8]

  Other measures of outcome frequency that will be discussed later, but are useful for nominal data include prevalence and incidence.[3] (see pages 46-47)

		Mean	**Median**	**Mode**
Parametric	**Interval, Ratio**	+	+	+
Non-Parametric	**Ordinal**	-	+	+
	Nominal	-	-	+
Sensitive to outliers		+	-	-

Gaussian or **normally distributed data.**[2,7,8,15]

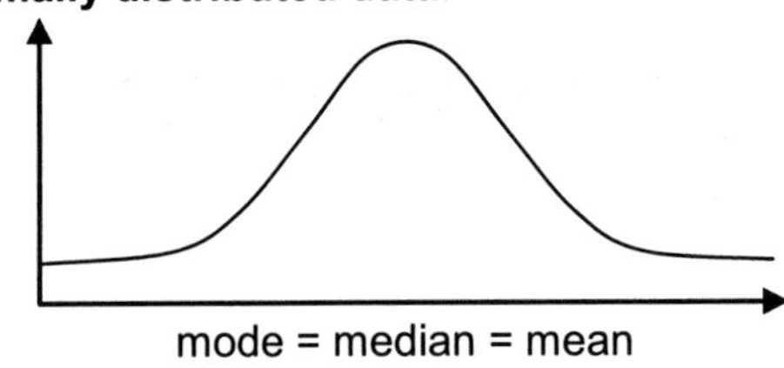

Positively skewed data: mode< median<mean [2,7,8]

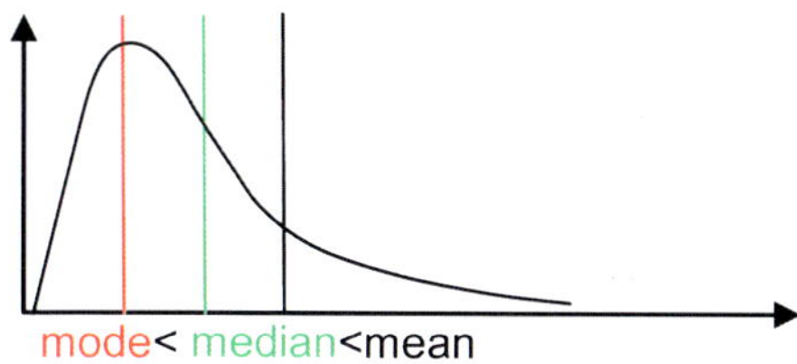

Negatively skewed data: mode>median>mean [2,7]

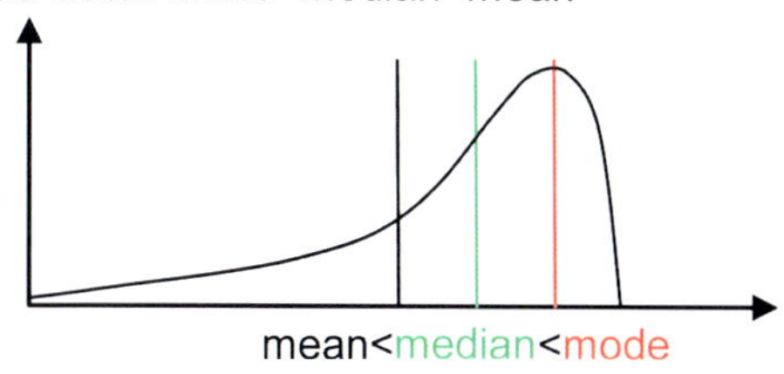

This is important because, based upon a data set's mean, median, and mode values, one can determine if the data are normally distributed or skewed when no graphical representation is provided.

Measures of central tendency do not describe variability or spread of data and may be misleading without some idea of data spread which leads us to our next topic, measures of variability.

Measures of Variability

These describe data spread and, in the case of confidence intervals (CIs), may help one infer if study groups differ significantly or if they were drawn from different populations.[2]

- **Range**: interval between lowest and highest values.[2,7,8,15] It only considers extreme values, so it is affected by outliers.[2,8,15] It is descriptive only, so is not used to infer statistical significance.[2]

- **Interquartile Range**: interval between the 25th and 75th percentiles, so it is directly related to median, or the 50th percentile.[2,11,15] It is not affected by outliers and, along with the median, is used for ordinal scale data.[2,11]

- **Variance**: deviation from the mean, expressed as the square of the units used. The data are squared in the variance calculation because some deviations are negative and squaring provides a positive number.[2,7] "As n increases, variance decreases."[11] Variance = sum of (Mean – data point) squared, divided by n–1

  $$\text{Variance} = \frac{[\sum (\bar{X} - X_1)^2]}{n - 1}$$

- **Standard Deviation (SD)**: square root of variance.[2,7,11] SD estimates the degree of data scatter around the sample mean.[15] 68% of data lies within ± 1SD of the mean and 95% of data lies within ± 2SD of the mean.[2,7,8,11,15] SD is only meaningful when data are normally or near-normally distributed and therefore is only applicable to parametric data.[2,7,8,11,15] Sigma (σ) is the population SD and S is the sample SD.[7]

  $$SD = \sqrt{\text{variance}}$$

- "**Coefficient of variation** (aka relative standard deviation): The coefficient of variation is another measure used when evaluating dispersion from one data set to another. The coefficient of variation is the SD expressed as a percentage of the mean. This is useful in comparing the relative difference in variability between two or more samples – or which group has the largest relative variability of values from the mean."[15] The smaller the coefficient of variation, the less the variability in the data set.

  $$\text{Coefficient of variation} = 100 \times SD/\bar{X}$$

- **Standard Error of the Mean (SEM)** [aka Standard Error (SE)]: SD divided by the square root of n.[2,7,8,15] The larger n is, the smaller SEM is.[2,7] SEM is always smaller than SD.[15] "Separate samples from a single population will give slightly different parameter estimates. The distribution of means from random samples is approximately normal. The mean of this 'distribution of means' is the unknown population mean."[7,8] SD for this distribution of means is estimated by the SEM.[8] So one "could name the SEM as the 'standard deviation of means of random samples of a fixed size drawn from the original population of interest.'"[15]

  A more simplistic way of explaining it is that the SEM is the quantification of the spread of the sample means for a study that is repeated multiple times. So it helps estimate how well a sample represents the population from which it was drawn.[7]

SEM **should not be used as a measure of variability when publishing a study.** Doing so is misleading. The only purpose of SEM is to calculate confidence intervals (CI), which contain an estimate of the true population mean from which the sample was drawn.[2] Therefore, **if one is provided SEM as a measure of variability for a study, he/she should use this only in calculating SD** and/or CIs to provide a more accurate, and less misleading, estimate of sample variability.[2]

$SEM = SD/\sqrt{n}$

- **Confidence Interval (CI)**: method of **estimating the range of values likely to include the true value of a population parameter.**[2] In medical literature, a 95% CI is most frequently used. The 95% CI is a range of values that, "**if the entire population could be studied**, 95% of the time **the true population value** would fall within the CI estimated from the sample."[2] For a 95% CI, 5 times out of 100, the **true population** parameter may not lie within the CI. For a 97.5% CI, 2.5 times out of 100, the true population parameter may not lie within the CI. Therefore, a 97.5% CI is more likely to include the true population value than a 95% CI.[2]

The true strength of a CI is that it is both **descriptive and inferential**. "All values contained in the CI are statistically possible."[8] However, the closer the point estimate lies to the middle of the CI, the more likely the point estimate represents the population.[15]

E.g., If a point estimate and 95% CI for mortality are 0.81 (95% CI: 0.63-0.99), all values including and between 0.63-0.99 are statistically possible. However, a point estimate of 0.79 is a more accurate representation of the studied population than a point estimate of 0.64 since 0.79 is closer to the sample's point estimate of 0.81 than is 0.64. As seen in this example, CI shows the degree of certainty (or uncertainty) in each comparison in an easily interpretable way.

In addition, CIs make it easier to assess clinical significance and **are less likely to mislead one into thinking that non-significantly different sample values imply equal population values.**

$95\%CI = \bar{X} +/- 1.96\ (SEM)$

Significance of CIs depends upon the objective of the trial one is conducting or evaluating.

Different Types of objectives include:

- **Superiority Trials** test if the efficacy of an experimental medication is "superior" or "inferior" to that of a control group; the control may be placebo or an active, standard of care, treatment control. Superiority trials are **the gold standard study design for most fields of clinical study since they have the most concrete boundaries for detecting differences between evaluated groups**.

- **Equivalence Trials** test if the efficacy of an experimental treatment (e.g., medication) is "sufficiently similar" to that of an active treatment control, to "justify use" of the experimental treatment.[20] **Pre-defined equivalence margins (aka thresholds) are based upon prior studies** (usually placebo controlled & sometimes only one study) **that tested the efficacy of the active treatment control. Unless otherwise specified, equivalence margins pertain solely to the primary endpoint of a study, rather than secondary, tertiary, or safety endpoints.**

- **Non-Inferiority Trials** test if the efficacy of an experimental treatment (e.g., medication) is "not clinically inferior" to that of an active treatment control.[20] The **pre-defined non-inferiority margin (aka threshold) is based upon prior studies** (usually placebo controlled & sometimes only one study) **that tested the efficacy of the active treatment control.** The non-inferiority margin is usually the smallest value considered to be clinically meaningful and usually less than half of the endpoint difference between the active treatment control and placebo.[20,34] **Unless otherwise specified, the non-inferiority margin pertains solely to the primary endpoint of a study, rather than secondary, tertiary, or safety endpoints.**

SUPERIORITY TRIALS test if the efficacy of an experimental medication is "superior" or "inferior" to that of a control group; the control may be placebo or an active, standard of care, treatment control. Superiority trials are **the gold standard study design for most fields of clinical study since they have the most concrete boundaries for detecting differences between evaluated groups**.

How to evaluate CI when endpoints of a study are RATIOS:

Examples of RATIOS include the following:

- **Relative Risk (RR) (aka Risk Ratio)**
- **Odds Ratio (OR)**
- **Hazards Ratio (HR)**

RR, OR, HR definitions and calculations are on pages 149-160.

Since all values within a CI are statistically possible, for outcomes that are ratios like RR, OR, and HR, if the 95% CI "excludes 1, the results are interpreted as being "statistically significant" (SS); either statistically significantly superior or statistically significantly inferior depending on the results relative to the control. If the 95% CI includes 1, the results are interpreted as being "not statistically significant" (NSS). This does not mean that the treatments are equal.

- **If the 95% CI excludes 1: SS**

- **If the 95% CI includes 1: NSS**

- **In the case of a 90% CI, if the CI includes ONE (1.0) for this type of data, it can be interpreted as a p>0.10.**[11,12,15]

- **In the case of a 95% CI, if the CI includes ONE (1.0) for this type of data, it can be interpreted as a p>0.05.**[11,12,15]

- **In the case of a 97.5% CI, if the CI includes ONE (1.0) for this type of data, it can be interpreted as a p>0.025.**[11,12,15]

In the following examples, point estimates (i.e., RR) and 95% CIs are represented as short vertical lines and attached horizontal lines, respectively.

Superiority Trial Table (modification of table[20])
Outcome: **Relative Risk for death**

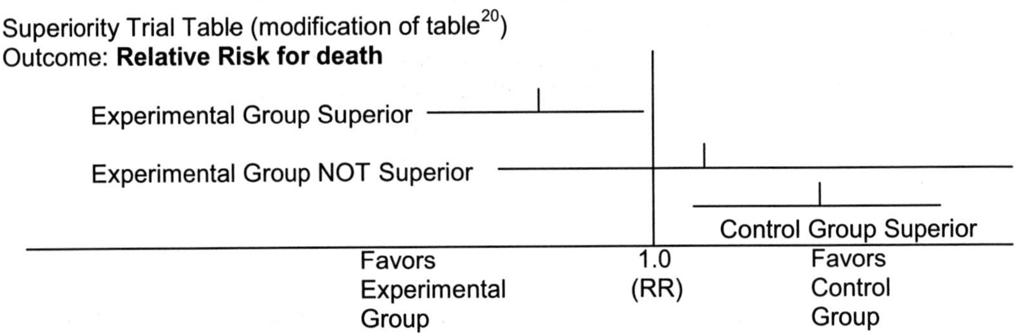

Superiority Trial Table (modification of table[20])
Outcome: **Relative Risk for clearing an infection**

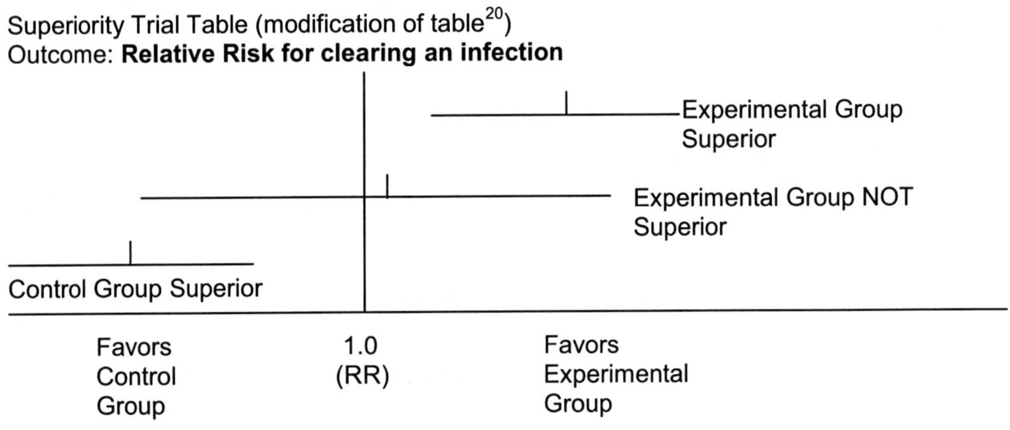

SUPERIORITY TRIALS continued:

How to evaluate CI when endpoints of a study are DIFFERENCES:

Examples of DIFFERENCES include the following:

- **Parametric data like BP reduction, cholesterol reduction, finger stick blood sugar (FSBS) or glycosylated hemoglobin (A1c) reductions**
- **Relative Risk Reductions (RRR) or Increases (RRI)**
- **Absolute Risk Reductions (ARR) or Increases (ARI)**

RRR, RRI, ARR, ARI definitions and calculations are on pages 149-156.

Since all values within a CI are statistically possible, for DIFFERENCES like RRR, RRI, ARR, ARI, blood pressure reduction or increase, A1c reduction or increase, etc., if the 95% CI "excludes ZERO (0), the results are interpreted as being "statistically significant" (SS); either statistically significantly superior or statistically significantly inferior depending on the results relative to the control. If the 95% CI includes ZERO (0), the results are interpreted as being "not statistically significant" (NSS). This does not mean that the treatments are equal.

- **If the 95% CI excludes 0: SS**

- **If the 95% CI includes 0: NSS**

- **In the case of a 90% CI, if the CI includes ZERO(0) for this type of data, it can be interpreted as a p>0.10.**[8,15]

- **In the case of a 95% CI, if the CI includes ZERO(0) for this type of data, it can be interpreted as a p>0.05.**[8,15]

- **In the case of a 97.5% CI, if the CI includes ZERO(0) for this type of data, it can be interpreted as a p>0.025.**[8,15]

In the following examples, point estimates (i.e., BP increase or decrease, HDL increase or decrease) and 95% CIs are represented as short vertical lines and attached horizontal lines, respectively.

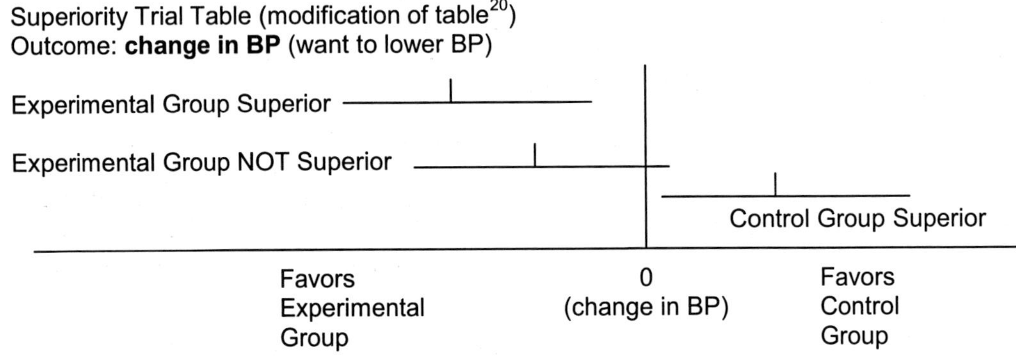

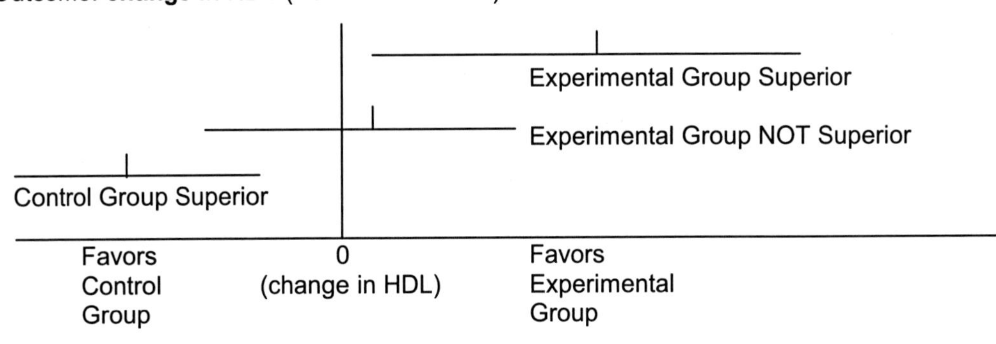

EQUIVALENCE TRIALS test if the efficacy of an experimental treatment (e.g., medication) is "sufficiently similar" to that of an active treatment control, to "justify use" of the experimental treatment.[20] **Pre-defined equivalence margins (aka thresholds) are based upon prior studies** (usually placebo controlled & sometimes only one study) **that tested the efficacy of the active treatment control. Unless otherwise specified, equivalence margins pertain solely to the primary endpoint of a study, rather than secondary, tertiary, or safety endpoints.**

If the 95% CI falls within and excludes BOTH margins of the "PRE-DEFINED EQUIVALENCE INTERVAL", the experimental medication is considered equivalent to the active treatment control medication. However, just as with superiority trials, if the 95% CI excludes 1 for ratios like RR, OR, and HR, or zero for differences like RRR, RRI, etc., the results are interpreted as being superior (or inferior depending on the results relative to the control).

If the 95% CI includes EITHER OR BOTH margins of the "PRE-DEFINED EQUIVALENCE INTERVAL", the experimental medication is NOT considered equivalent to the active treatment control medication.

In the following examples, point estimates (i.e., RR) and 95% CIs are represented as short vertical lines and attached horizontal lines, respectively.
Pre-defined equivalence margins are represented as vertical dotted lines.

Equivalency Trial Tables

Outcome: **Relative Risk for death**

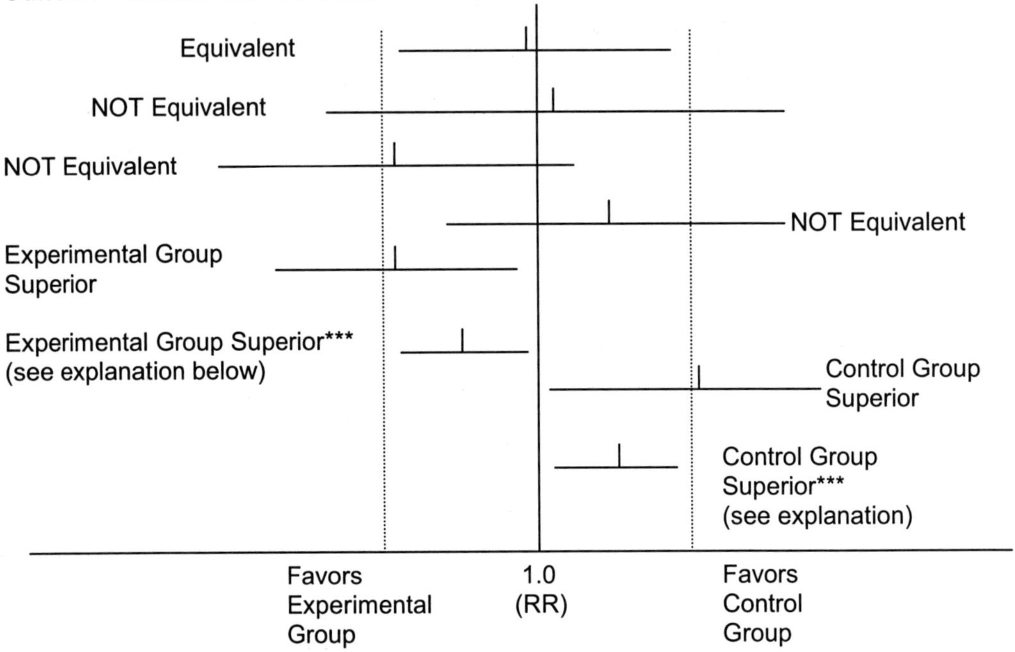

Equivalent

NOT Equivalent

NOT Equivalent

NOT Equivalent

Experimental Group Superior

Experimental Group Superior***
(see explanation below)

Control Group Superior

Control Group Superior***
(see explanation)

Favors Experimental Group

1.0 (RR)

Favors Control Group

***explanation: Technically speaking, the groups are equivalent since the 95% CI for the experimental group is within the predefined equivalency margins. However, remember that the equivalency margins are statistically generated margins rather than a finite margin like superiority. Therefore, in these types of cases, the results should be presented in terms of superiority.

Outcome: **Relative Risk for clearing an infection**

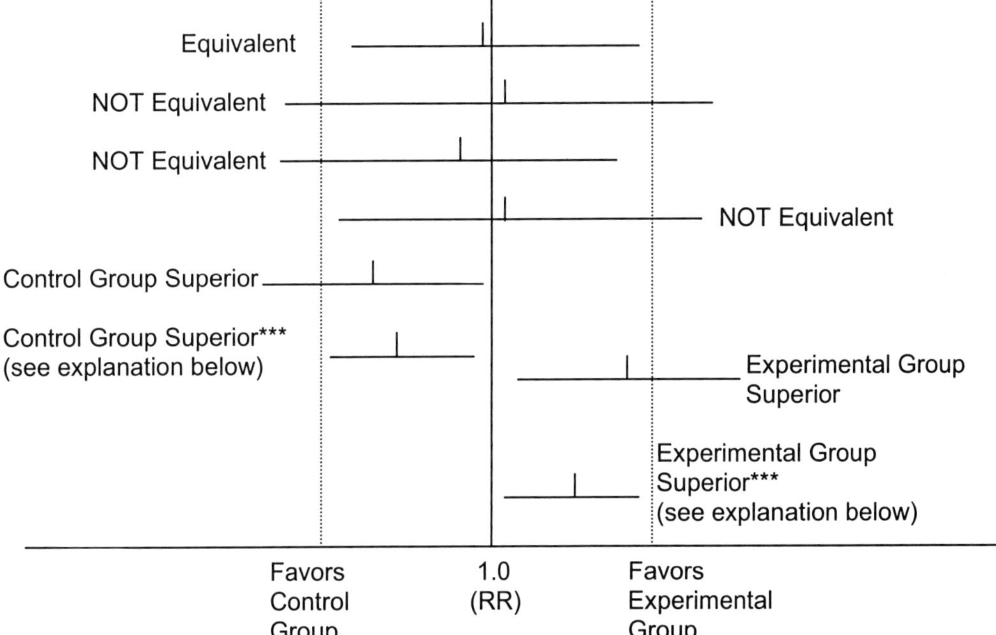

***explanation: Technically speaking, the groups are equivalent since the 95% CI for the experimental group is within the predefined equivalency margins. However, remember that the equivalency margins are statistically generated margins rather than a finite margin like superiority. Therefore, in these types of cases, the results should be presented in terms of superiority.

Weaknesses of Equivalence trials:

- Equivalence trials are much more problematic in terms of reliability of results than are superiority trials since weak internal validity is rewarded with bias towards equivalence.[34,40]

- **Analysis**

  - For equivalence trials, intention-to-treat (ITT: see pages166-168) analysis often leads to smaller effect sizes and, therefore, tends to bias towards no difference between the evaluated groups.[30,34,40] This "could make a truly inferior treatment appear to be equivalent"[30,34,40]

  - Per-protocol analysis (see page 169) could bias the results either towards or away from no difference between the evaluated groups.[30,34,40]

  - **Therefore <u>equivalence trials should be analyzed using both ITT and Per-protocol analyses, and ONLY if BOTH support equivalence are the results considered conclusive</u>.**[30,40]

NON-INFERIORITY TRIALS test if the efficacy of an experimental treatment (e.g., medication) is "not clinically inferior" to that of an active treatment control.[20] The **pre-defined non-inferiority margin (aka threshold) is based upon prior studies** (usually placebo controlled & sometimes only one study) **that tested the efficacy of the active treatment control. The non-inferiority margin is usually the smallest value considered to be clinically meaningful and usually less than half of the endpoint difference between the active treatment control and placebo.[20,34] Unless otherwise specified, the non-inferiority margin pertains solely to the primary endpoint of a study, rather than secondary, tertiary, or safety endpoints.**

If the 95% CI excludes the "PRE-DEFINED NON-INFERIORITY MARGIN" (aka THRESHOLD), the results are interpreted as non-inferior. However, just as with superiority trials, if the 95% CI excludes 1 for ratios like RR, OR, and HR, or zero for differences like RRR, RRI, etc., the results are interpreted as being superior (or inferior depending on the results relative to the control).

If the 95% CI includes the "PRE-DEFINED NON-INFERIORITY MARGIN" (aka THRESHOLD), the results are interpreted as NOT non-inferior.

In the following examples, point estimates (i.e., RR) and 95% CIs are represented as short vertical lines and attached horizontal lines, respectively.
Pre-defined non-inferiority margins are represented as vertical dotted lines.

Non-Inferiority Trial Tables (modification of table[20])
Outcome: **Relative Risk for death**

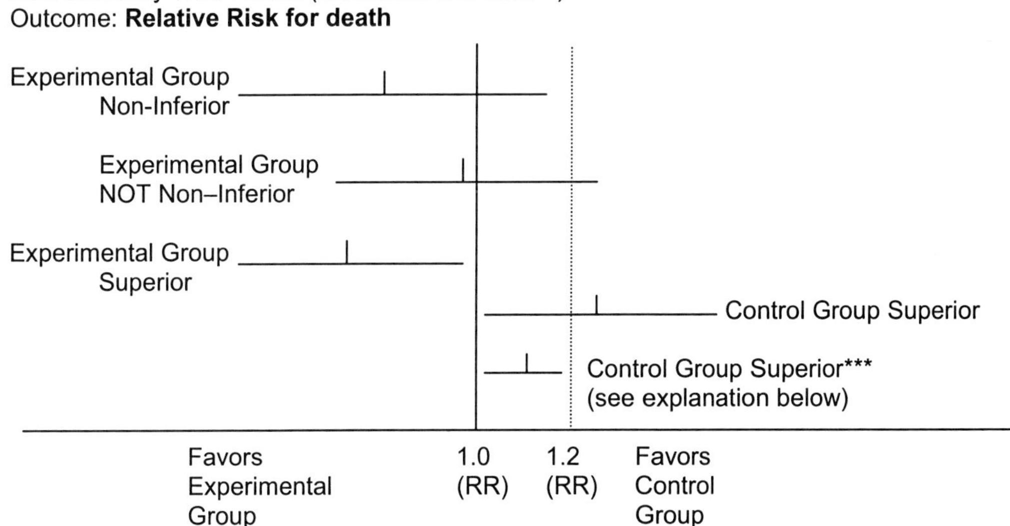

***explanation: Technically speaking, the experimental group is non-inferior since the 95% CI is below the predefined non-inferiority margin. However, remember that the non-inferiority margin is a statistically generated margin rather than a finite margin like superiority. Therefore, in these types of cases, the results should be presented in terms of superiority.

Non-Inferiority Trial Table (modification of table[20])
Outcome: **Relative Risk for clearing an infection**

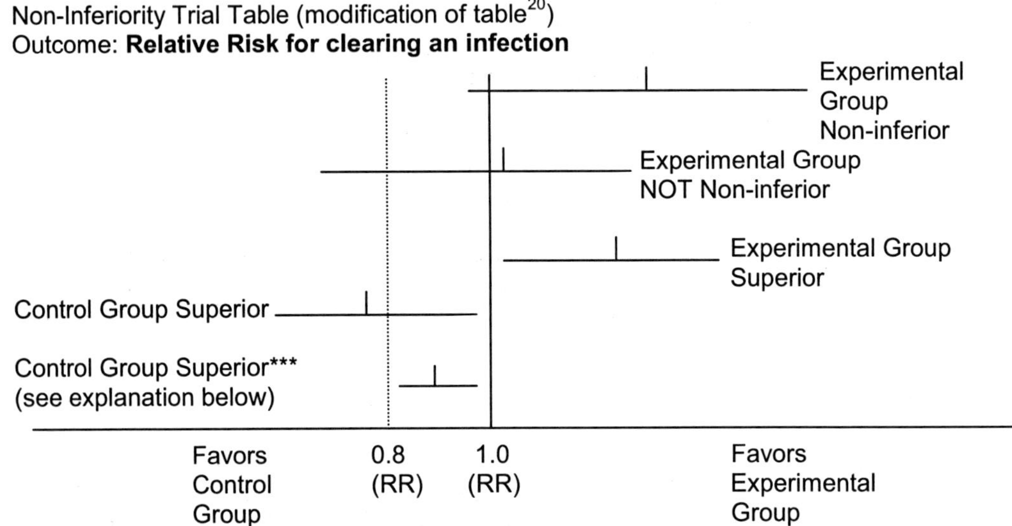

***explanation: Technically speaking, the experimental group is non-inferior since the 95% CI is above the predefined non-inferiority margin. However, remember that the non-inferiority margin is a statistically generated margin rather than a finite margin like superiority. Therefore, in these types of cases, the results should be presented in terms of superiority.

Weaknesses of Non-inferiority trials:

- Non-inferiority trials are much more problematic in terms of reliability of results than are superiority trials since weak internal validity is rewarded with bias towards non-inferiority.[34,40]
    - There is "no protection against blinded investigators' biasing the results toward a preconceived belief in non-inferiority by assigning similar ratings to the treatment responses of all patients."[30]
    - "Discontinuations can obscure a true treatment effect."[30]
- **Analysis**
    - For non-inferiority trials, ITT analysis (see pages 166-168) often leads to smaller effect sizes and, therefore, tends to bias towards no difference between the evaluated groups.[30,34] This "could make a truly inferior treatment appear to be non-inferior."[30,34]
    - Per-protocol analysis (see page 169) could bias the results either towards or away from no difference between the evaluated groups.[30,34]
    - **Therefore <u>non-inferiority trials should be analyzed using both ITT and Per-protocol analyses, and ONLY if BOTH support non-inferiority are the results considered conclusive</u>.**[30]

Study Questions: (provided by Melanie Pound, PharmD, BCPS)

6. Which of the following can be described by all 3 measures of central tendency?
   a. History of diabetes
   b. Mortality
   c. NYHA Classification
   d. Ejection fraction

7. Which of the following data can be described in terms of mode only (and NOT in terms of median or mean)?
   a. Mortality
   b. Difference in blood pressure
   c. Number of cigarettes smoked daily
   d. NYHA classification

8. Which measure(s) of central tendency is/are sensitive to outliers?

9. All of the following data can be described in terms of mean, median and mode EXCEPT:
   a. History of diabetes
   b. Phenytoin serum concentration
   c. Cholesterol concentrations
   d. Heart rate

10. Which of the following can be accurately described by the median and mode ONLY and NOT by the mean?
    a. NYHA classification
    b. Ejection fraction
    c. Mortality
    d. History of CVA

11. For what type of data can standard deviation be used?

12. Which of the following is correct regarding measures of variability?
    a. Range can be both descriptive and inferential.
    b. SEM is always larger than SD.
    c. All values contained in the CI are statistically possible.
    d. CI is a descriptive measure only.

13. Which of the following is NOT correct regarding measures of variability?
    a. The range is descriptive ONLY.
    b. The SD is ALWAYS less than the SEM.
    c. The SEM is ALWAYS less than the SD.
    d. The CI is considered both descriptive and inferential.

14. OASIS V compared enoxaparin to fondaparinux for patients with acute coronary syndrome. The non-inferiority margin was pre-defined as 1.185 for the primary endpoint of death, MI, or refractory ischemia at 9 days. The Hazard Ratio for the primary endpoint was 1.01 (95% CI: 0.90 - 1.13). Based upon these results, which of the following conclusions can be made regarding the primary endpoint:
    a. Fondaparinux is statistically significantly different from enoxaparin because the CI crosses 1.
    b. Fondaparinux is non-inferior to enoxaparin because the upper limit of the CI is less than 1.185.
    c. Fondaparinux is statistically significantly different from enoxaparin because the CI is less than 1.185.
    d. Fondaparinux is non-inferior because the CI crosses 1.

15. If the above trial had been a superiority trial, how would that have changed the interpretation of the results of the primary endpoint?
    a. Fondaparinux is statistically significantly different from enoxaparin because the CI exceeds 0.
    b. Fondaparinux is statistically significantly different from enoxaparin because the CI includes 1.
    c. Fondaparinux is NOT statistically significantly different from enoxaparin because the CI exceeds 0.
    d. Fondaparinux is NOT statistically significantly different from enoxaparin because the CI includes 1.

16. For which of the following studies would either a standard treatment control or an equivalence trial design be more appropriate than a placebo-control design?
    a. Treatment of hypertension in hypertension-induced stroke patients
    b. Treatment with a statin in post-MI patients
    c. Treatment of bacterial pneumonia patients
    d. A standard treatment control or equivalence trial design would be acceptable for all of the above scenarios.

17. Which of the following is CORRECT regarding measures of variability?
    a. Although the range is easy to compute, it is inferential only.
    b. The SEM is always less than the SD.
    c. Although all values in the CI are clinically possible, they are not always statistically possible.
    d. The CI provides descriptive information only.

18. All of the following would be appropriate for a superiority trial design EXCEPT:
    a. Warfarin vs. placebo for stroke prevention in atrial fibrillation (Afib) patients with heart failure, DM and h/o CVA.
    b. Candesartan + standard of care vs. standard of care for heart failure with reduced ejection fraction (HFrEF) patients.
    c. Chlorthalidone 6.25-25mg daily vs hydrochlorothiazide (HCTZ) 6.25-25mg daily for blood pressure control and clinical outcomes in adult patients with stage 1 hypertension.
    d. Spironolactone + standard of care vs. eplerenone + standard of care for HFrEF patients.
    e. Moderate to high dose simvastatin vs. moderate to high dose atorvastatin for atherosclerotic cardiovascular disease (ASCVD) endpoint prevention in type 2 diabetes.

(For the next 2 questions) Use the Forrest Plots below:

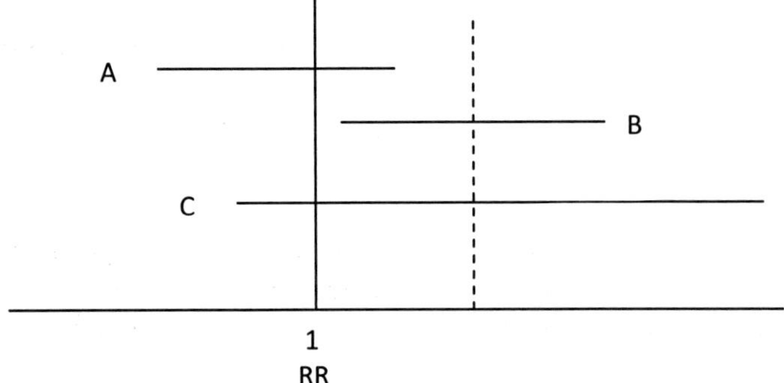

19. Based on the above Forrest Plots, which of the following lines demonstrates non-inferiority if the endpoint being evaluated is "risk of death or hospitalization"? The upper limit of the non-inferiority boundary is represented by the dotted vertical line.
    a. A
    b. B
    c. C
    d. Both A & B

20. If the above Forrest Plots were representative of a superiority trial evaluating efficacy in "clearing of an infection" with a new antibiotic, which of the following lines represents superiority?
    a. A
    b. B
    c. C
    d. Both A & C

21. A recent trial studied “Oral rivaroxaban for symptomatic venous thromboembolism (VTE)” (N Engl J Med 2010;363:2499-2510). In this trial, rivaroxaban was compared with enoxaparin-VKA regimen. The upper limit of the non-inferiority margin was set at 2.0 for the primary outcome which was recurrent VTE. The results are listed in the table below.

Efficacy	**Rivaroxaban**	**Enoxaparin-VKA**	**HR (95% CI)**
Recurrent VTE	2.1%	3.0%	0.68 (0.44-1.04)
Major bleeding	0.8%	1.2%	0.65 (0.33-1.30)
Mortality	2.2%	2.9%	0.67 (0.44-1.02)

What can be concluded about the primary endpoint?

a. Rivaroxaban is non-inferior to enoxaparin-VKA because the CI includes 1.
b. Rivaroxaban is non-inferior to enoxaparin-VKA because the CI does not include 0.
c. Rivaroxaban is non-inferior to enoxaparin-VKA because the CI does not include 2.0.
d. Rivaroxaban is superior to enoxaparin-VKA because the CI does not include 2.0.

(For the next 2 questions)
In the RE-LY trial, dabigatran was compared with warfarin for the prevention of CVA in Afib patients. The primary outcome in this trial was CVA or systemic thromboembolism. In this trial, for dabigatran to be considered non-inferior to warfarin, the 95% CI must not exceed 1.46 for the primary outcome. The results are presented below.

Endpoint	Dabigatran 150 mg (n=6076)	Warfarin (n=6022)	RR, 95% CI
CVA or systemic embolism	134 (2.2%)	159 (2.6%)	0.66 (0.53-0.82)
CVA	122 (2.0%)	185 (3.1%)	0.64 (0.51-0.81)
MI	89 (1.5%)	63 (1.0%)	1.38 (1.00-1.91)

22. What can be concluded about the primary endpoint?
    a. Dabigatran is non-inferior to warfarin because the CI does not include 1.
    b. Dabigatran is superior to warfarin because the CI does not include 1.
    c. Dabigatran is non-inferior to warfarin because the CI does not include 0.
    d. Dabigatran is superior to warfarin because the CI does not include 0.

23. What can be included about the outcome "MI"?
    a. Dabigatran has a higher MI risk than warfarin, although it is not statistically significant because the CI includes 1.
    b. Dabigatran has a higher MI risk than warfarin, although it is not statistically significant because the CI does not include 0.
    c. Dabigatran has a higher MI risk than warfarin and it is statistically significant because the CI includes 1.
    d. Dabigatran has a higher MI risk than warfarin and it is statistically significant because the CI does not include 0.

Answers to Study Questions:

6. d - Only parametric data can be described by all 3 measures of central tendency: mean, median, and mode. Ejection fraction is parametric data since it is scored on a continuum with a consistent level of magnitude of difference between data units. Mortality and history of diabetes are nominal since they are yes/no questions. NYHA classification is ordinal since it is scored on a continuum but there is not a consistent level of magnitude of difference between the data points.

7. a - Nominal data are the only type of data that can only be described by mode. Mortality is nominal. Difference in blood pressure and number of cigarettes smoked are parametric. NYHA classification is ordinal.

8. Mean is the only measure of central tendency that is affected by outliers. Neither median nor mode is affected by outliers.

9. a - Only parametric data can be described by all 3 measures of central tendency: mean, median, and mode. Of the four choices, only history of diabetes is not parametric. Rather, it is nominal.

10. a - Only ordinal data can only be described by median and mode. NYHA classification is ordinal. Ejection fraction is parametric and therefore can be described by mean, median, and mode. Mortality and history of CVA are nominal and can only be described by mode.

11. Standard deviation can only be used for parametric (aka continuous) data.

12. c - All values contained in the CI are statistically possible. Range is only descriptive. It is not inferential. SEM is always smaller than SD. CI is descriptive and inferential.

13. b – SEM is always smaller than SD. Range is only descriptive. CI is descriptive and inferential.

14. b - Since the upper limit of the CI for the primary endpoint does not include the NI margin (1.185), Fondaparinux is non-inferior to enoxaparin. (see below)

Primary Outcome: **death, MI, or refractory ischemia at 9 days**

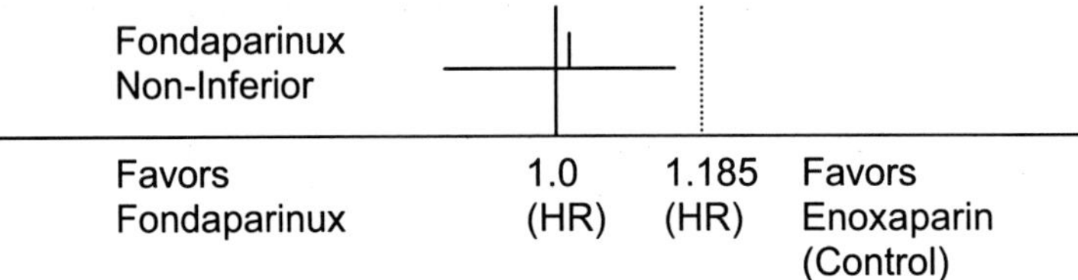

If the upper limit of the CI for the primary endpoint were below 1.0, Fondaparinux would have been deemed as being superior to enoxaparin. (see below)

Fondaparinux
Superior

Favors Fondaparinux | 1.0 (HR) | 1.185 (HR) | Favors Enoxaparin (Control)

If the lower limit of the CI for the primary endpoint were above 1.0, enoxaparin would have been deemed as superior to Fondaparinux. (see below)

Enoxaparin
Superior

Favors Fondaparinux | 1.0 (HR) | 1.185 (HR) | Favors Enoxaparin (Control)

15. d - Since the CI includes 1.0, there is no statistically significant difference between Fondaparinux and enoxaparin. (see below)

Primary Outcome: **death, MI, or refractory ischemia at 9 days**

Fondaparinux
Not superior

Favors Fondaparinux | 1.0 (HR) | Favors Enoxaparin (Control)

16. d - Since we have data supporting the use of standard of care agents for all of the scenarios, using a placebo control design would be unethical in all of these scenarios. A standard treatment control would be most appropriate for the hypertension and statin trials. For the pneumonia trial, either a standard treatment control trial or an equivalence design utilizing a standard of care antibiotic would be appropriate.

17. b - The SEM is always less than the SD. Range is not inferential; it is descriptive only. All values in the CI are statistically possible. The CI provides descriptive and inferential information.

18. a - Since we have data supporting the use of standard of care agents to minimize the risk of stroke in Afib patients with heart failure, DM and h/o CVA, it would be unethical to use a placebo control. A standard treatment control would be necessary in this case. All of the other trial scenarios would be ethical to conduct as of 2014.

19. a - Since the primary outcome is risk of death or hospitalization, the upper limit of the CI for the primary endpoint would need to be below the NI margin (vertical dotted line) to determine non-inferiority of the experimental group. (see below)

Primary Outcome: **death or hospitalization**

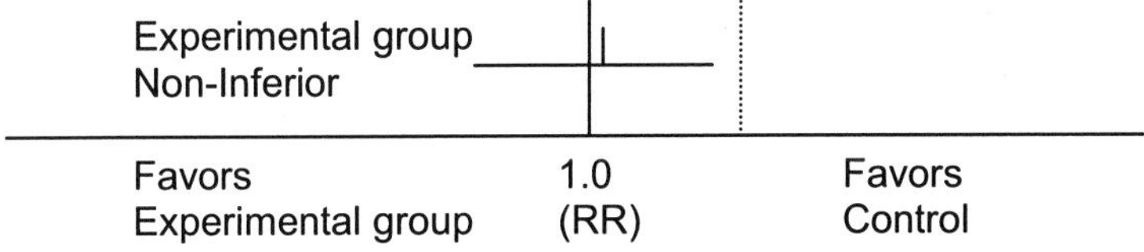

If the primary outcome were something like clearing of an infection or cure of a disease, the lower limit of the CI for the primary endpoint would need to be above the NI margin to determine non-inferiority of the experimental group. (see below)

Primary Outcome: **cure of a disease**

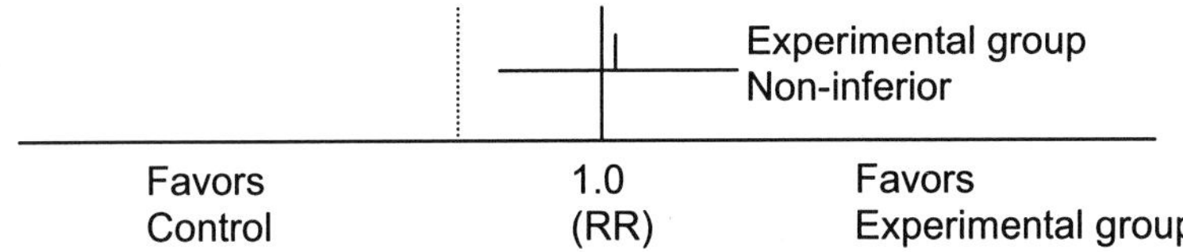

20. b - Since the endpoint is clearing an infection, the lower limit of the CI for the endpoint would need to be above 1.0 to establish superiority of the experimental group. (see below)

Primary Outcome: **clearing an infection**

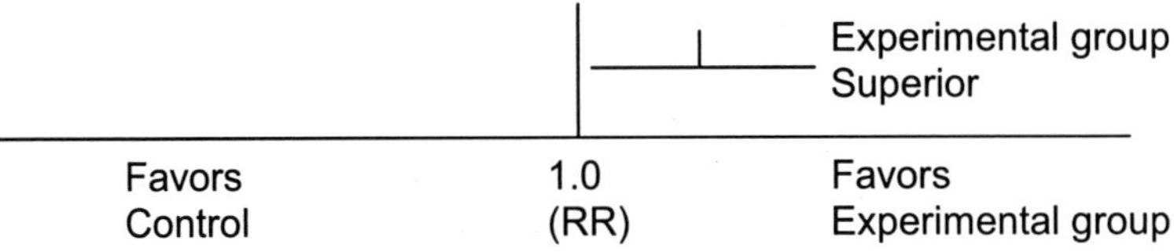

Favors Control	1.0 (RR)	Favors Experimental group

If the endpoint were something like death or hospitalization, the upper limit of the CI for the endpoint would need to be below 1.0 to establish superiority of the experimental group. (see below)

Primary Outcome: **hospitalization**

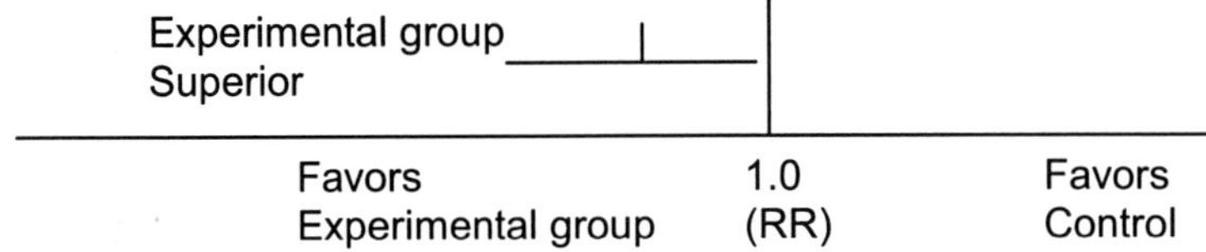

Favors Experimental group	1.0 (RR)	Favors Control

21. c - Rivaroxaban is non-inferior to enoxaparin-VKA because the CI does not include 2.0. (see below)

Primary Outcome: **Recurrent VTE**

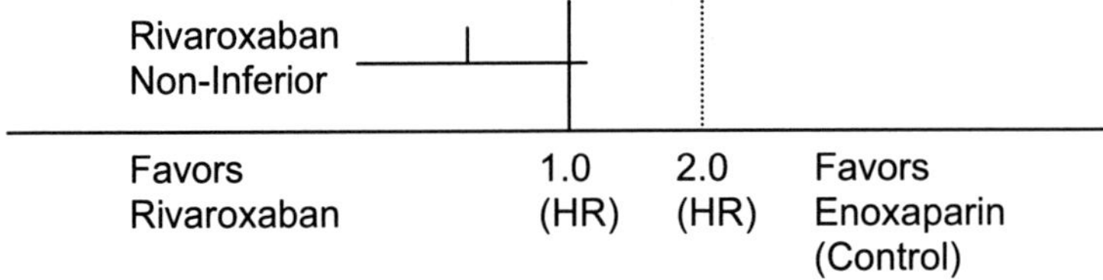

Favors Rivaroxaban	1.0 (HR)	2.0 (HR)	Favors Enoxaparin (Control)

22. b - Dabigatran is superior to warfarin because the CI does not include 1.

Since the endpoint is CVA or systemic embolism, the upper limit of the CI would need to be below 1.0 for dabigatran to be superior to warfarin. (see below)

Primary Outcome: **Recurrent VTE**

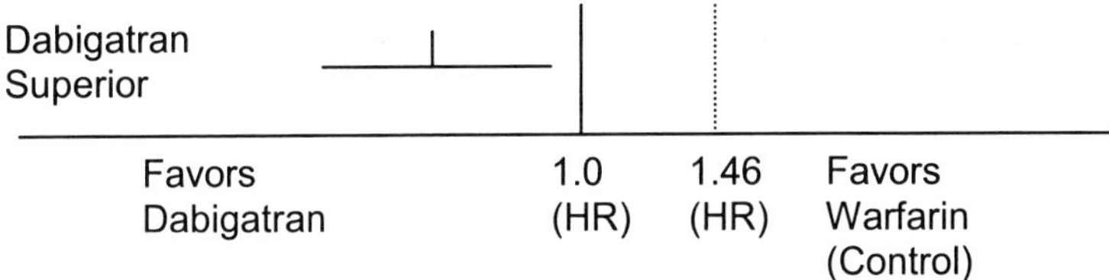

Favors Dabigatran | 1.0 (HR) | 1.46 (HR) | Favors Warfarin (Control)

23. a - Dabigatran has a higher MI risk than warfarin. Since the CI includes 1.0, the difference is not statistically significant. However, this does not mean the higher MI risk is not clinically important. In fact, this is one of the reasons many clinicians have avoided using Dabigatran in AFib patients despite the 2012 Chest guideline recommendations to do so.

Secondary Outcome: **MI**

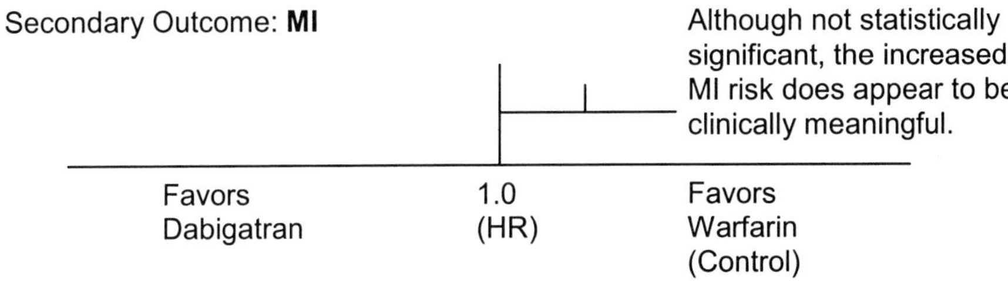

Part 3: Sensitivity, Specificity, Predictive Value, and Hypothesis Testing[3]

Sensitivity and Specificity are used to measure validity of screening/diagnostic tests.[3]

- **Sensitivity**: the ability of a test to reliably detect the **presence** of disease.[3,12]
- **Specificity**: the ability of a test to reliably detect the **absence** of disease.[3,12]

Most new diagnostic tests are evaluated in relation to another older, previously accepted, often more invasive, and historically reliable test (i.e., the gold standard test).[3,12]
For the purposes of this discussion, assume that the results obtained by the gold standard test are always correct.[3]

For the following examples, FP = false positive, FN = false negative, TP = true positive, and TN = true negative.

Example 1 from Gaddis & Gaddis Part 3:[3]
New MRI venogram vs. gold standard intravenous contrast venogram.[3]

Of 250 patients suspected of having a DVT, only 150 actually had a DVT as detected by the gold standard IV contrast venogram. Therefore, 100 of the 250 suspected patients did not have a DVT. (250-150 = 100)[3]

The new MRI test detected a DVT in 130 of the 150 patients who actually had a DVT. (130 TP). So there were 20 patients who the new MRI test incorrectly classified as being DVT-free.[3] (150-130 = 20 FN)

The new MRI test classified 87 of the 100 patients as DVT-free. (87 TN) So there were 13 patients in whom the new MRI test incorrectly detected the presence of DVT.[3] (100-87 = 13 FP)

		Gold Standard Test (Presence of Disease)		
		Present	Absent	Totals
New Test Result	Positive	**TP**	FP	**TP + FP**
	Negative	FN	**TN**	**TN + FN**
	Totals	**TP + FN**	**TN + FP**	**TP + FP + TN + FN**

Adapted from reference 41

		Gold Standard Test (Presence of Disease)		
		Present	Absent	Totals
New Test Result	Positive	**130 TP**	13 FP	**143 TP + FP**
	Negative	20 FN	**87 TN**	**107 TN + FN**
	Totals	**150 TP + FN**	**100 TN + FP**	**250 TP + FP + TN + FN**

Adapted from reference 41

Now for the good stuff: 1) calculation of the ability of this new MRI test to reliably detect the **presence** of disease (**Sensitivity**) and 2) calculation of the ability of this new MRI test to reliably detect the **absence** of disease (**Specificity**).

- **Sensitivity** (%) = 100 x TP/(TP + FN) = 100 x 130/(130+20) = 86.7%. So this New MRI test is 86.7% reliable in detecting a DVT when it is actually present.[3]

- **Specificity** (%) = 100 x TN/(TN +FP) = 100 x 87/(87+13) = 87%. So this New MRI test is 87% reliable in detecting absence of a DVT when it is actually absent.[3]

Since virtually no diagnostic tests are 100% specific and sensitive, **one canNOT use sensitivity or specificity to predict presence or absence of disease in patients.**

For this, one needs to utilize predictive values.

Predictive Values[3]

Predictive values are used to help predict the likelihood of disease in an individual patient.[3]

- **Positive predictive value (PPV): the proportion of patients with disease when presence of disease is indicated by the diagnostic test.**[3,12]
For this example, PPV = 100 x TP/(TP+FP) = 100 x 130/(130+13) = 90.9% [3,12]

- **Negative predictive value (NPV): the proportion of patients free of disease when absence of disease is indicated by the diagnostic test.**[3,12]
For this example, NPV = 100 x TN/(TN+FN) = 100 x 87/(87+20) = 81.3% [3,12]

Note that if you set your table up correctly, **sensitivity and specificity are calculated along verticals** whereas **positive and negative predictive values are calculated using horizontals of the graph**.

PPV and NPV are affected by prevalence of disease.[3]

Prevalence

Prevalence is the proportion of a population with disease at a specific point in time. Another definition of prevalence is the number of people with disease at any point in time divided by the total number of people at risk of having that disease.[3,11]

Prevalence (%) = 100x (TP+FN)/(n) -OR- 100x (TP+FN)/(TP+FP+TN+FN).
For our DVT example, since there were 150 patients with DVT out of 250 patients tested, the prevalence = 100 x 150/250 = 60% [3]

> **This is not to be confused with incidence (aka cumulative incidence) which is the number of _new cases_ that occur during a specified time period divided by the number of subjects initially followed to detect the outcome of interest.**[3,11]
>
> $$\text{Incidence} = \frac{\text{\# of new cases}}{\text{persons}}$$
>
> May use person-time as the denominator instead of number of persons. (One individual followed for 3 years represents 3 person-years of follow-up.)[3]
>
> $$\text{Incidence} = \frac{\text{\# of new cases}}{\text{person-years}}$$

Table 2 of Gaddis and Gaddis[3] **helps in understanding** the statement made earlier **that PPV and NPV are affected by the prevalence of disease** in the population.[3]
As prevalence of a disease decreases, PPV (the proportion of patients with disease when presence of disease is indicated by the diagnostic test) **will also decrease** and the **NPV** (the proportion of patients free of disease when absence of disease is indicated by the diagnostic test) **will increase.**[3]

The converse is also true; as prevalence of disease increases, PPV will also increase, and NPV will decrease.

Comparing PPV and NPV in examples 1 and 2 will help in understanding this concept. (see example 2 below)

Example 2: [3]
In this example 200 patients are at risk for having a DVT.
Prevalence of disease is 20%, so 200 x 0.20 = 40 patients with DVT.[3]

In example 1, we found that the new MRI test had a sensitivity of 86.7%. So one can reliably detect the presence of a DVT in 86.7% of the 40 DVT patients.
0.86 x 40 = 35patients, so 35 patients are TP and 40 – 35 = 5 patients are FN.[3]

In example 1, we found that the new MRI test had a specificity of 87%. So one can reliably detect the absence of a DVT in 87% of the 160 DVT-free patients.
0.87 x 160 = 139 patients, so 139 patients are TN and 160-139 = 21 patients are FP.[3]

		Gold Standard Test (Presence of Disease)		
		Present	Absent	Totals
New Test Result	Positive	**35** **TP**	21 FP	**56** **TP + FP**
	Negative	5 FN	**139** **TN**	**144** **TN + FN**
	Totals	**40** **TP + FN**	**160** **TN + FP**	**200** **TP + FP + TN + FN**

Adapted from reference 41

In the example 2 population,

PPV = 100 x TP/(TP+FP) = 100 x 35/(35+21) = 62.5% and...

NPV = 100 x TN/(TN+FN) = 100 x 139/(139+5) = 96.5%.[3]

Therefore, as prevalence decreased from 60% (example 1) to 20% (example 2), PPV decreased from 90.9% to 62.5% and the NPV increased from 81.3% to 96.5%, respectively.[3]

Based upon this example, one can see that a new diagnostic test's usefulness will depend upon the prevalence of disease in the particular population being evaluated.[3] For example, the usefulness of a particular test will depend upon the geographical location and population in which it will be used.

Example:
One would expect prevalence of human immunodeficiency virus (HIV) positive persons in Haiti to be higher than the prevalence of HIV+ persons in Maine.

Knowing this, one would be more likely to believe a positive HIV test for a person in Haiti than for a person living in Maine.

Conversely, one would also be more likely to believe a negative HIV test for a person in Maine than for a person living in Haiti.

So, basically one is saying the same thing with PPV and NPV.

For PPV: The proportion of individuals with HIV in Haiti when a particular test detects presence of disease would be expected to be higher than if that same test were to be used in Maine.

For NPV: The proportion of individuals without HIV in Haiti when a particular test detects absence of disease would be expected to be lower than if that same test were to be used in Maine.

Hypothesis Testing

- **H_o (null hypothesis)**: For superiority trials, H_o is that no difference exists between studied populations.[3,8,11]

- **H_1 (alternative hypothesis)**: For superiority trials, H_1 is that a difference does exist between studied populations.[3,11] H_1 is usually directional. For example, investigators may expect a 15% reduction on cardiovascular mortality or a 10% increase in clearing an infection.

The null hypothesis is tested instead of the alternative hypothesis **because there are an infinite number of alternative hypotheses.** It would be **impossible to calculate the required statistics for each of the <u>infinite number of possible magnitudes of difference</u> between population samples H_1 hypothesizes.**[3]

H_o is used to determine "if any observed differences between groups are due to chance alone" or sampling variation.[8]

Statistical significance is tested (hypothesis testing) to indicate if H_o should be accepted or rejected.[3,8,12]

- For superiority trials, if H_o is "rejected" = statistically significant difference between groups exists (results unlikely due to chance)[3,8,12]

- For superiority trials, if H_o is "accepted" = NO statistically significant difference exists.[3,8,12] NOTE: "Failing to reject H_o is not sufficient to conclude that groups are equal."[27]

For **Superiority Trials**: Modification of Table 3 on page 146/592[3]

	Reality	
	Difference Exists (H_o False)	No Difference Exists (H_o True)
Decision from Stat Test		
Difference Found (Reject H_o)	Correct No error	Incorrect **Type 1** error (false positive)
No Difference Found (Accept H_o)	Incorrect **Type 2** error (false negative)	Correct No error

Type 1 error occurs **if one rejects H_o when, in fact, H_o is true.**[3,11] For superiority trials, a type 1 error occurs if one detects a difference between treatment groups, when in fact, no difference exists.[3,8,11,12]

Alpha (α) is defined as the probability of making a Type 1 error.[3,11,12] When α level is set *a priori* (or before the trial), H_o is rejected when $p \le \alpha$.[3,8] By convention, α is usually 0.05 (5%), which means that 1 time out of 20, a Type 1 error will be committed. This is a consequence that investigators are willing to accept and is denoted in trials as a $p \le 0.05$.[3,8,11,12]

So the p-value is the calculated chance that a type 1 error has occurred.[3,8,12] In other words, it tells us the likelihood of obtaining a statistically significant result if H_o were true. "At p=0.05, the likelihood is 5%. At p=0.10, the likelihood is 10%."[8]

$p \le \alpha$ means the observed treatment difference is statistically significant, it does not indicate the size or direction of the difference.[8] The size of the p-value is NOT related to the importance of the result.[6,8,17] Smaller p-values only mean that "chance" is less likely to explain observed differences.[6,8,17] Also, "a small p-value does not correct for systematic error (bias)" from a poorly designed study.[27]

Type 2 error occurs if one **accepts H_o when, in fact, H_o is false.**[3,8,11,12] For superiority trials, a type 2 error occurs if no difference is detected between treatment groups, when in fact, a difference does exist.[11,12]

Beta (β) is the probability of making a Type 2 error.[3,11,12] By convention, β is 0.2 (20%) or less.[3,8,11]

For **Equivalence and Non-inferiority Trials**: "the null and alternative hypotheses are reversed" because H_o is opposite.[34,40]

As seen in the graph below, for a superiority trial, exclusion of the superiority boundary means that a difference exists between the groups. For a non-inferiority or equivalence trial, exclusion of the non-inferiority or equivalence boundarie(s) means that a difference does not exist.

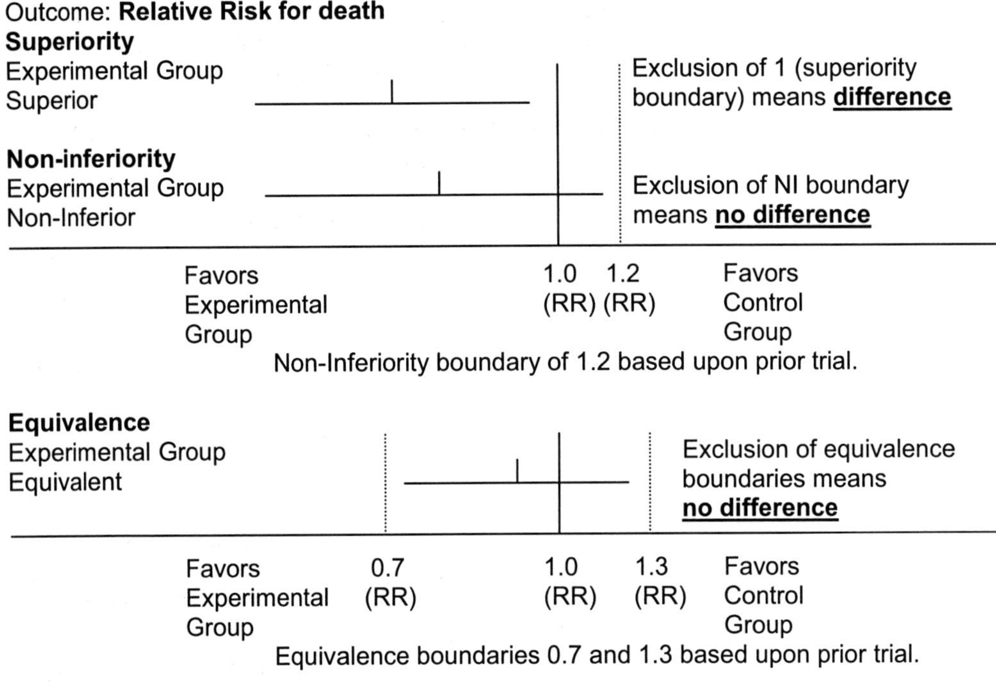

Therefore, type 1 error and type 2 error are the exact opposite for equivalence and non-inferiority trials than for superiority trials.

	Reality for NI or Equivalence Trial	
	Difference Exists (H_o True)	No Difference Exists (H_o False)
Decision from Stat Test		
Difference Found (Accept H_o)	Correct No error	Incorrect **Type 2** error (false negative)
No Difference Found (Reject H_o)	Incorrect **Type 1** error (false positive)	Correct No error

When evaluating efficacy endpoints of superiority trials, which is worse, Type 1 vs Type 2 error?

- Examples:
    - If a trial indicates that Drug X decreases stroke risk, when it actually doesn't affect stroke risk. (type 1 error) What will happen?
        - Clinicians will stop using aspirin and/or clopidogrel and start using Drug X. In this case, effective anti-stroke medication(s) will be replaced with an ineffective medication. Pretty bad mistake, huh?
    - Another trial indicates that Drug Y does not decrease stroke risk, when it actually does decrease stroke risk. (type 2 error) What will happen?
        - In this case patients will remain on aspirin and/or clopidogrel, which also decrease risk for stroke.
- Which error is more acceptable? Just think about the conventionally accepted percentages for type 1 and 2 errors.
    - For most trials, only a 5% chance of making a type 1 error is acceptable.
    - For most trials, up to a 20% chance of making a type 2 error is acceptable.

Regardless of the trial design (superiority, equivalence, or non-inferiority), α and β are interrelated.[3] All else held constant, α and β are inversely related.[3] In other words, as α is decreased, β is increased and as α is increased, β is decreased. (i.e., as risk for a Type 1 error is increased, risk for a Type 2 error is decreased and vice versa).[3] The **most common use of β is in calculating the approximate sample size needed to keep α and β acceptably small.**[3]

Power is the ability of an experiment to detect a statistically significant **difference** between samples, when in fact, a significant difference truly exists.[3,8,11,12] Said another way, power is the probability of making a correct decision when H_o is false.[11]

- **Power = 1- β**

Parametric tests are generally more precise, and therefore, more powerful than non-parametric tests.[3] Correct study design and statistical tests increase power to detect true differences. Poor study design and incorrect statistical tests decrease power to detect true differences.[3,8]

For superiority trials, inadequate power may cause one to conclude that no difference exists when, in fact, a difference does exist (type 2 error).[3]

Note that in most cases, power is an issue only if one accepts H_o. If one rejects H_o there is no way that one could have made a type 2 error.

For **Superiority Trials**: Modification of Table 3 on page 146/592 [3]

	Reality	
	Difference Exists (H_o False)	No Difference Exists (H_o True)
Difference Found (Reject H_o)	**Correct No error**	**Incorrect Type 1 error (false positive)**
No Difference Found (Accept H_o)	Incorrect Type 2 error (false negative)	Correct No error

Therefore, power to detect a difference would **not** be an issue in most of these cases. An exception to this general rule would be if one wanted to decrease data variability or spread. For example, if one wanted to narrow the 95% CI, increasing power by increasing sample size could help.

Power calculations are used to either:

- Determine the power of a study to detect a certain effect after the study has been completed, as is done when evaluating articles for journal clubs.[11,12,16]
- Determine sample size needed when designing a study (i.e., prior to the study), usually based upon the primary endpoint. It is important to note that patients drop out of trials. So when calculating sample size, calculate the completion count to help ensure an adequate number of patients will complete the trial.[11,12,16]

Sample Size Completion Count

Sample size (corrected for drop out) $= \dfrac{\textbf{number of patients}}{\textbf{1 – percent of expected drop outs as a decimal}}$

Let's say that 30% of patients in each group will drop out. If one originally calculated the need for 123 patients in each group to reach 80% power to detect a 25% relative difference between the 2 groups....

Sample size (corrected for drop outs) $= \dfrac{123}{(1 - 0.3)} = \dfrac{123}{0.7} =$ **175.7 (i.e., 176 patients needed in each group to reach 80% power to detect a 25% relative difference between the 2 groups)**

Delta (Δ) is also known as "effect size". Delta is the degree of difference between tested samples.[3]

Website that can be used for calculation of sample size and power
www.stat.ubc.ca/~rollin/stats/ssize/

One-tailed vs Two-tailed tests: It is easier to show a statistically significant difference with a one-tailed test than with a two-tailed test, because **with a one-tailed test** a statistical test **result need *not* vary as much from the mean** to achieve significance at any level of α chosen.[3,15]

Most reputable journals require that investigators perform statistics based upon a two-tailed test even if it innately makes sense that a difference would only occur uni-directionally.[11,12,18]

In the following examples, the red arrows represent the 95% CI boundaries.

Example 1: Superiority Trial

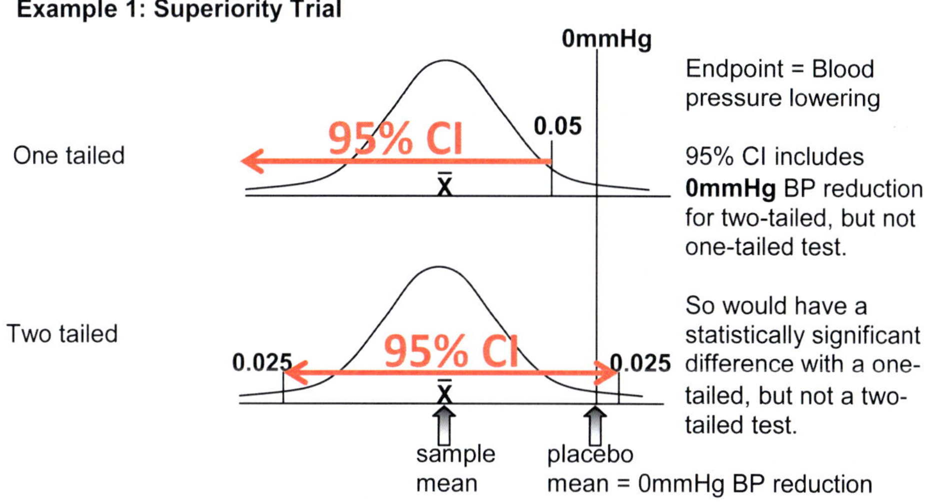

Example 2: Superiority Trial

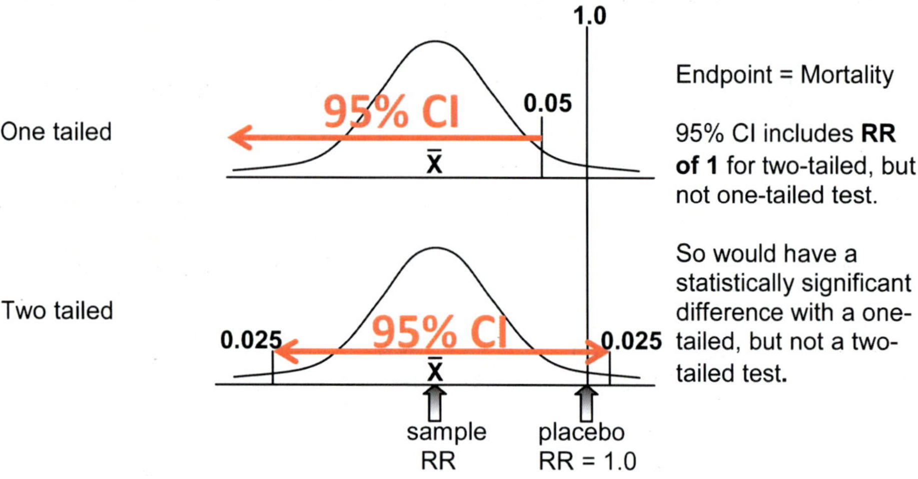

Example 3: Non-inferiority Trial

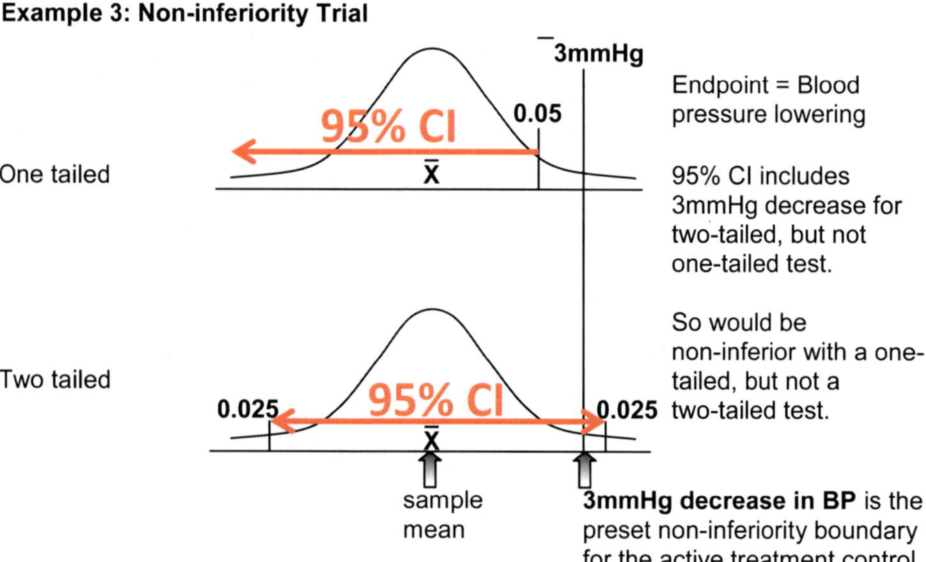

Note: To help minimize type 1 error risk, many reputable journals currently require non-inferiority trials to utilize a one-tailed alpha risk of 0.025 or 2.5% (i.e., a one-tailed 97.5% CI).

Example 4: Non-inferiority Trial

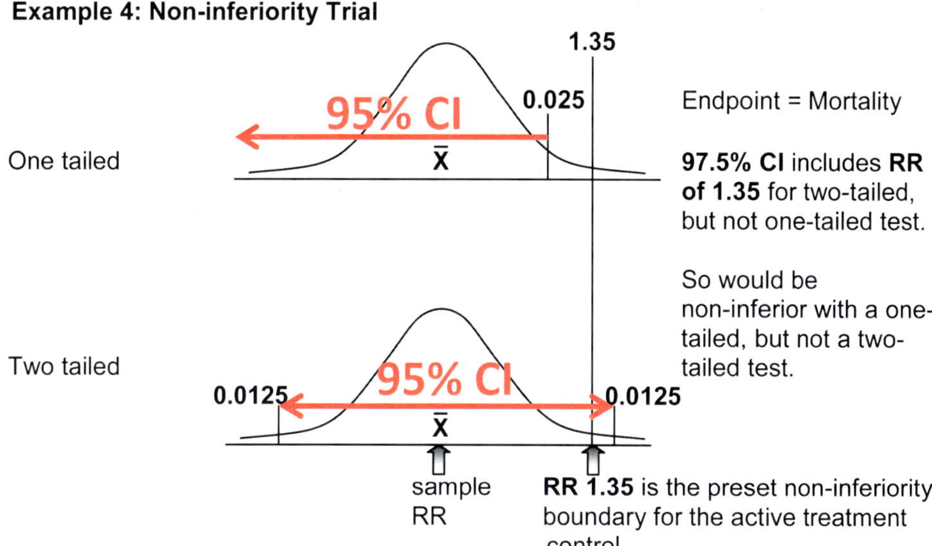

Note that for all of the sample size calculation examples on the following pages, a one-tailed test requires a smaller sample size than a two-tailed test to detect differences between groups.

How α, β, Δ, tailing (1-tailed vs 2-tailed), and incidence affect sample size required for nominal outcomes data. The following tables, examples, and explanations were provided by Richard Drew, PharmD, MS, BCPS

ONE-TAILED VS TWO-TAILED[16]

Incidence		Statistical Limits		Sample Size	
Expected incidence (%)	Difference b/n groups (Δ in %)	α	β	**One-tailed test**	**Two-tailed test**
40	10	0.05	0.20	**1820**	**2310**
10	10	0.05	0.20	**10,630**	**13,495**

For a given α error risk, a one-tailed test requires a smaller sample size than a two-tailed test to detect differences between groups.

EFFECT OF **CHANGE IN ALPHA (α)**[16]

Incidence		Statistical Limits		Sample Size	
Expected incidence (%)	Δ (%)	α	β	One-tailed test	Two-tailed test
80	10	**0.05**	0.20	351	446
80	10	**0.10**	0.20	256	351

Increasing the acceptable type 1 (α) statistical error risk will decrease the sample size required.

Decreasing the acceptable type 1 (α) statistical error risk will increase the required sample size.

EFFECT OF **CHANGE IN BETA (β)**[16]

Incidence		Statistical Limits		Sample Size	
Expected incidence (%)	Δ (%)	α	**β**	One-tailed test	Two-tailed test
80	10	0.05	**0.20**	351	446
80	10	0.05	**0.40**	205	279

Increasing the acceptable type 2 (β) error risk will decrease the sample size required. Said another way, smaller sample sizes increase type 2 (β) error risk if the α limit is fixed.

Decreasing the acceptable type 2 (β) error risk will increase the sample size required. Said another way, larger sample sizes decrease type 2 (β) error risk if the α limit is fixed.

Since power = 1- β, a smaller sample size decreases power and a larger sample size increases power.

EFFECT OF **CHANGE IN DELTA (**Δ: difference between groups)[16]

Incidence		Statistical Limits		Sample Size	
Expected incidence (%)	**Δ (%)**	α	β	One-tailed test	Two-tailed test
80	**10**	0.05	0.20	351	446
80	**20**	0.05	0.20	96	122
80	**50**	0.05	0.20	17	22

A smaller difference (Δ) increases the sample size required to detect that difference.

A larger difference (Δ) decreases the sample size required to detect that difference.

EFFECT OF **CHANGE IN EXPECTED INCIDENCE**[16]

Incidence		Statistical Limits		Sample Size	
Expected incidence (%)	Δ (%)	α	β	One-tailed test	Two-tailed test
10	10	0.05	0.20	10,630	13,495
40	10	0.05	0.20	1820	2310
80	10	0.05	0.20	351	446

A smaller incidence increases the sample size required to detect differences between groups. This is why so many trials combine endpoints.

A larger incidence decreases the sample size required to detect differences between groups.

For parametric data, α, β, Δ, and tailing (1 vs 2 tailed) affect required sample size the same way as is exemplified in the nominal data examples above. However, with parametric endpoint data, standard deviation (SD) is used to calculate sample size rather than incidence.

EFFECT OF **CHANGE IN STANDARD DEVIATION (SD)**

Differences		Statistical Limits		Sample Size	
SD	Δ (%)	α	β	One-tailed test	Two-tailed test
1 (68% of data)	10	0.05	0.20	1237	1570
2 (95% of data)	10	0.05	0.20	4947	6280

Utilizing a more inclusive (i.e., larger) standard deviation (SD) will require a larger sample size.

Website that can be used for calculation of sample size and power for nominal and parametric data.

www.stat.ubc.ca/~rollin/stats/ssize/

Statistically vs Clinically Significant Difference

Statistically significant differences do not necessarily translate into clinically significant differences.[3,8] If the sample size of a study is large enough, non-clinically meaningful, statistically significant differences may be detected.

> For example, with a large enough sample size, one may detect a statistically significant difference between one blood pressure medication which decreases systolic blood pressure by 10mmHg and another blood pressure medication which decreases systolic blood pressure by 11mmHg. Although statistically significant, this difference would not be clinically meaningful.

Also, lack of statistical significance does not necessarily mean the results are not clinically significant. (consider power, study design, and populations studied)[6,8] A non-statistically significant difference is more likely to be accepted as being clinically significant in the instance of safety issues (like adverse effects), than for endpoint improvements.

> For example, if a study were to find a non-statistically significant increase in the risk for invasive breast cancer with a particular medication, many clinicians may deem this as being clinically meaningful such that they would avoid using the agent until further data were obtained.

<u>**Judging the clinical significance of a statistically significant difference**</u>[27, 28]

Determine what others think is clinically significant by:

- Considering the effect used in the sample size calculation (if reported).[27, 28]
- Considering existing evidence-based or expert consensus statements.[27, 28]
- Considering any cost-effectiveness or decision analyses that have been performed.[27, 28]

Absent such guidance, require that the minimum worthwhile effect be large when:

- The intervention is costly (e.g., in terms of time, money, or other resources).[27, 28]
- The intervention is high risk.[27, 28]
- The outcome is unimportant, or has intermediate importance but with uncertain benefit to patients.[27, 28]
- A patient is risk-averse.[27, 28]

Accept the minimum worthwhile effect as small when:

- The intervention is low-cost.[27, 28]
- The intervention is low risk.[27, 28]
- The intervention is important and has an unambiguous outcome (e.g., death).[27, 28]
- A patient is risk-taking.[27, 28]

Prior Probability: consistency with previous work.[3]

Example 1: High prior probability
Angiotensin converting enzyme inhibitors (ACEIs) have been used to treat systolic dysfunction heart failure for years based upon multiple, randomized, controlled trials which support their ability to improve clinical outcomes. Therefore ACEIs exhibit high prior probability for treating heart failure. So there is a low risk for making a type 1 error, but a high risk of making a type 2 error when ACEIs are tested for treating heart failure.

Example 2: Low prior probability
Acetaminophen has never demonstrated effectiveness for heart failure. Therefore acetaminophen exhibits low prior probability for treating heart failure. So there is a high risk for making a type 1 error, but a low risk for making a type 2 error when acetaminophen is tested for treating heart failure.

Study Questions: (provided by Rebekah Grube, PharmD, BCPS)

(for the next 5 questions) A new diagnostic test (serum Aspergillus antigen test) is being developed to detect the presence of invasive aspergillosis (IA) in lung transplant patients more rapidly than the "gold standard" of cultures. In a recent study of the utility of this new diagnostic test, 497 subjects were tested using conventional cultures as well as serum Aspergillus antigen tests. Of these 497 subjects, 120 had a positive serum antigen test and positive cultures; 40 had positive serum antigen tests and negative cultures; 97 subjects had negative serum antigen tests and positive cultures; and 240 had negative serum antigen tests and negative cultures. (For the purposes of this test, assume that results of the gold standard are always correct)

24. Which of the following statements is true regarding the Aspergillus antigen test given the information above?
    a. The serum Aspergillus antigen test is 55% reliable in detecting the presence of IA when it is actually present.
    b. The serum Aspergillus antigen test is 71% reliable in detecting the presence of IA when it is actually present.
    c. The serum Aspergillus antigen test is 75% reliable in detecting the presence of IA when it is actually present.
    d. The serum Aspergillus antigen test is 86% reliable in detecting the presence of IA when it is actually present.

25. Which of the following statements is true regarding the Aspergillus antigen test given the information above?
    a. The serum Aspergillus antigen test is 55% reliable in detecting the absence of IA when it is actually absent.
    b. The serum Aspergillus antigen test is 71% reliable in detecting the absence of IA when it is actually absent.
    c. The serum Aspergillus antigen test is 75% reliable in detecting the absence of IA when it is actually absent.
    d. The serum Aspergillus antigen test is 86% reliable in detecting the absence of IA when it is actually absent.

26. Which of the following statements is true given the information above?
    a. A patient with a negative serum Aspergillus antigen has a 55% chance of not actually having IA.
    b. A patient with a negative serum Aspergillus antigen has a 71% chance of not actually having IA.
    c. A patient with a negative serum Aspergillus antigen has a 75% chance of not actually having IA.
    d. A patient with a negative serum Aspergillus antigen has an 86% chance of not actually having IA.

27. Which of the following statements is true given the information above?
    a. A patient with a positive serum Aspergillus antigen has a 55% chance of actually having IA.
    b. A patient with a positive serum Aspergillus antigen has a 71% chance of actually having IA.
    c. A patient with a positive serum Aspergillus antigen has a 75% chance of actually having IA.
    d. A patient with a positive serum Aspergillus antigen has an 86% chance of actually having IA.

28. Based upon the above study, what is the calculated prevalence of invasive aspergillosis (IA)?
    a. 24%
    b. 44%
    c. 48%
    d. 56%

29. The manufacturers of the serum Aspergillus antigen decide to investigate the use of the test in heart and lung transplant patients, which have a higher prevalence of IA. Which of the following statements is correct regarding the effects of prevalence on the usefulness of the test?
    a. The reliability of the antigen to accurately detect the absence of IA will increase.
    b. The reliability of the antigen to accurately detect the absence of IA will decrease.
    c. The percentage of patients that actually have IA when the antigen test is positive will increase.
    d. The percentage of patients that actually have IA when the antigen test is positive will decrease.
    e. Both “b” and “d” are correct

(for the next 3 questions) A study was performed to determine the effect of a new antipsychotic agent (Hallucigone®) on psychosis in patients with underlying schizophrenia as compared to placebo. A sample size of 300 patients was calculated to be needed based upon an alpha of 0.05 and a beta of 0.20. The double-blind, parallel, superiority trial was performed in 350 patients for 8 weeks. At the end of the 8-week period, the new antipsychotic agent was found to induce remission in 20% of patients as compared to 18% in the placebo group (p=0.07).

30. Which of the following statements best reflects the alternative hypothesis for the above study (before the study is conducted)?

    I. Hallucigone® will induce significantly more remissions of psychosis than placebo in patients with schizophrenia.
    II. Hallucigone® will induce significantly fewer remissions of psychosis than placebo in patients with schizophrenia.
    III. Hallucigone® will not significantly induce a different number of remissions of psychosis in patients with schizophrenia than placebo.

    a. I only
    b. II only
    c. III only
    d. I and II only

31. Which of the following statements is true based upon the results of the above study?
    a. Hallucigone® was found to have a statistically significant and clinically significant difference on remission of psychosis as compared to placebo.
    b. Hallucigone® was found to have a statistically significant difference but not a clinically significant difference on remission of psychosis as compared to placebo.
    c. Hallucigone® was found to have a clinically significant difference but not a statistically significant difference on remission of psychosis as compared to placebo.
    d. Hallucigone® was not found to have a clinically or statistically significant difference on remission of psychosis as compared to placebo.

32. Which of the following statements is NOT true regarding the power calculation for the above study?
    a. Utilizing a two-tailed test instead of a one-tailed test would have increased the sample size needed in the study.
    b. Increasing acceptable alpha apriori will increase the risk of making a type 2 error.
    c. Increasing the estimated difference between remission rates of Hallucigone® and placebo would have decreased the sample size needed.
    d. Utilizing incorrect statistical tests would decrease the power of the study.

33. The same investigators want to perform a follow-up study using a higher dose of Hallucigone®. They calculate that a sample size of 400 subjects (200 in each arm) will be needed to show a difference (based upon an alpha of 0.05 and beta of 0.20). They predict that given the patient population, approximately 50% of subjects will drop out of the study. Based upon the drop-out rate, how many subjects will be needed in each treatment arm?
    a. 100 subjects
    b. 200 subjects
    c. 400 subjects
    d. 800 subjects

34. *(For the next 2 questions)* A study was performed to determine the effect of a new blood pressure medication, Camelpril®, on blood pressure control as compared to chlorthalidone. A sample size of 2500 patients was calculated to be needed based upon an alpha of 0.025 and a beta of 0.10. The double-blind, parallel, superiority trial was performed in 2750 patients for 8 weeks. At the end of the 8-week period, Camelpril® was found to decrease blood pressure by 15mmHg as compared to 13mmHg with the chlorthalidone group (p=0.07). Which of the following statements is true regarding the power calculation for the above study?
    a. Utilizing a two-tailed test instead of a one-tailed test would have decreased the sample size required in the study.
    b. Changing alpha apriori to 0.05 will decrease the risk of making a type I error.
    c. A larger difference in the blood pressure lowering abilities between Camelpril® and chlorthalidone would have increased the sample size required to detect a statistically significant difference.
    d. Utilizing an inappropriate test would increase the power of the study.
    e. Increasing beta apriori will decrease the ability to find a difference when a difference truly exists.

35. The same investigators want to conduct a follow-up study using a higher dose of the new blood pressure medication Camelpril®. They calculate that a sample size of 2000 subjects (1000 in each arm) will be needed to show a difference (based upon an alpha of 0.025 and beta of 0.10). They predict that given the patient population, approximately 15% of subjects will drop out of the study. Based upon the drop-out rate, what is the least amount of subjects that will be needed in each treatment arm?
    a. 1100 subjects in each treatment arm
    b. 1200 subjects in each treatment arm
    c. 1250 subjects in each treatment arm
    d. 1300 subjects in each treatment arm
    e. 1335 subjects in each treatment arm

36. A group of investigators wants to evaluate a new medication for the treatment of thromboembolic stroke. They would like to conduct this trial as efficiently and inexpensively as possible WITHOUT compromising usual trial design standards. Which of the following would help decrease the number of patients required for their trial?
    a. Conduct the trial in a region with a higher incidence of thromboembolic stroke.
    b. Conduct the trial using an alpha of 2.5% rather than an alpha of 5%.
    c. Conduct the trial using a beta of 5% rather than a beta of 10%.
    d. Conduct the trial using conservative estimates for delta. (i.e., err on the side of a smaller rather than a larger delta)

37. A superiority trial evaluating a new cholesterol medication, Zetia, was stopped early b/c, although Zetia lowered LDL better than the active control niacin, the Zetia group had more negative cardiovascular outcomes like heart attack and death. There were 200 patients in this trial and differences were statistically and clinically significant. Which of the following is true?
    a. The trial was underpowered.
    b. The result may have been a delta error.
    c. The result may have been a Type 1 error.
    d. Power was possibly an issue with this trial.

38. A group of investigators wants to evaluate a new medication for the treatment of thromboembolic stroke. They would like to conduct this trial as efficiently and inexpensively as possible WITHOUT compromising usual trial design standards. Which of the following would help decrease the number of patients required for their trial?
    a. Conduct the trial in a region with a lower incidence of thromboembolic stroke.
    b. Conduct the trial using an alpha of 5% rather than an alpha of 2.5%.
    c. Conduct the trial using a beta of 10% rather than a beta of 20%.
    d. Conduct the trial using conservative estimates for delta. (i.e., err on the side of a smaller rather than a larger delta)

Answers to Study Questions:

		Gold Standard Test (Presence of Disease)		
		Present	Absent	Totals
New Test Result	Positive	**120 TP**	40 FP	**160 TP + FP**
	Negative	97 FN	**240 TN**	**337 TN + FN**
	Totals	**217 TP + FN**	**280 TN + FP**	**497 TP + FP + TN + FN**

Adapted from reference 41

Sensitivity = 100 x TP/(TP + FN) = 120/217 = 55%

Specificity = 100 x TN/(TN +FP) = 240/280 = 86%

PPV = 100 x TP/(TP+FP) = 120/160 = 75%

NPV = 100 x TN/(TN+FN) = 240/337 = 71%

Prevalence = 100x (TP+FN)/(n) **--OR--** 100x (TP+FN)/(TP+FP+TN+FN)
= 217/497
= 44%

24. a - This question is asking for sensitivity (ability to reliably detect presence of disease). Sensitivity = 100 x TP/(TP + FN) = 120/217 = 55%

25. d - This question is asking for specificity (ability to reliably detect absence of disease). Specificity = 100 x TN/(TN +FP) = 240/280 = 86%

26. b - This question is asking for NPV (likelihood of the patient's not having a disease when absence of disease is detected by the diagnostic test).
NPV = 100 x TN/(TN+FN) = 240/337 = 71%

27. c - This question is asking for PPV (likelihood of the patient's having disease when it is detected by the diagnostic test). PPV = 100 x TP/(TP+FP) = 120/160 = 75%

28. b - Prevalence = 100x (TP+FN)/(n) -OR- 100x (TP+FN)/(TP+FP+TN+FN)
= 217/497 = 44%

29. c - Sensitivity and specificity of a test are not affected by prevalence. PPV and NPV are affected by prevalence. As prevalence of disease increases, PPV will also increase, and NPV will decrease. The converse is also true; as prevalence of disease decreases, PPV will also decrease, and NPV will increase.

30. d

31. d - Since p of 0.07 is greater than the preset alpha of 0.05, the results are not statistically significant. Since there is a very small difference in the remission rate between Hallucigone and placebo, the results are not clinically meaningful; practice will not be changed to utilize Hallucigone since the risks of using this new medication with an unknown adverse effect profile outweigh the very small benefit.

32. b - Increasing acceptable alpha apriori will increase the risk of making a type 1 error, not a type 2 error. All of the other statements are true.

33. c - 200 in each arm/(1-0.5) = 200/0.5 = 400 in each treatment arm. If the question had asked how many total subjects would be needed (i.e., both arms), the answer would have been 400/(1-0.5) = 400/0.5 = 800.

34. e - Beta is the risk of committing a type 2 error (not detecting a difference when one truly exists). In this example, beta is 0.10 or 10%. Power is the ability to detect a difference between groups when one truly exists. Power = 1-beta = 1-0.10 = 90%.Therefore, increasing beta apriori (e.g. from 0.10 to 0.2) will decrease power (e.g., 1-0.2 = 0.8 or 80%). So increasing beta from 0.10 to 0.20 will decrease power from 0.90 or 90% to 0.80 or 80%. Conversely, decreasing beta apriori will increase power (the ability to find a difference when a difference truly exists). Utilizing a two-tailed test instead of a one-tailed test would have increased the sample size required in the study. Since this study's alpha is 0.025 or 2.5%, changing alpha apriori to 0.05 or 5% will increase the risk of making a type I error from 2.5% to 5%. A larger difference in the blood pressure lowering abilities (delta) between Camelpril® and chlorthalidone would have decreased the sample size required to detect a statistically significant difference. Utilizing an inappropriate test would decrease the ability of the study to detect true differences between groups (aka power).

35. b - 1000 in each arm/(1-0.15) = 1000/0.85 = 1176 patients would be needed for each arm and the closest rounded answer to choose from was 1200 subjects.

36. a - The higher the incidence of disease, the fewer patients needed to detect differences between groups when differences truly exist. Conducting the trial using an alpha of 2.5% rather than an alpha of 5% would increase the number of patients needed for the study. Conducting the trial using a beta of 5% rather than a beta of 10% would increase the number of patients needed for the study. Conducting the trial using conservative estimates for delta (i.e., erring on the side of a smaller rather than a larger delta), would increase the number of patients needed for the study.

37. c - Power is associated with beta: power = 1-beta. Beta is the risk of committing a type 2 error. If a statistically significant difference is detected, a type 2 error could not occur. Therefore the trial was not underpowered. With this scenario, there are only two possibilities: either 1) the findings were correct or 2) a type 1 error occurred.

38. b - Conducting the trial using an alpha of 5% rather than an alpha of 2.5% would decrease the number of patients needed for the study. The lower the incidence of disease, the more patients needed to detect differences between groups when differences truly exist. Conducting the trial using a beta of 10% rather than a beta of 20% would increase the number of patients needed for the study. Conducting the trial using conservative estimates for delta (i.e., erring on the side of a smaller rather than a larger delta), would increase the number of patients needed for the study.

Part 4: Statistical Inference Techniques in Hypothesis Testing[4]

Prior to going over these techniques, you will need to understand the difference between a parallel vs cross-over design and confounding.

Parallel design of the RCT is "preferred for acute diseases or for diseases in which treatment is curative."[29]

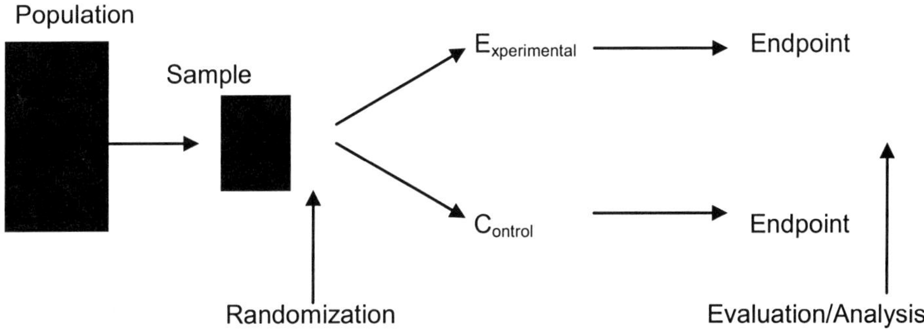

Cross-over design of the RCT is useful when there is wide, inter-patient variability.

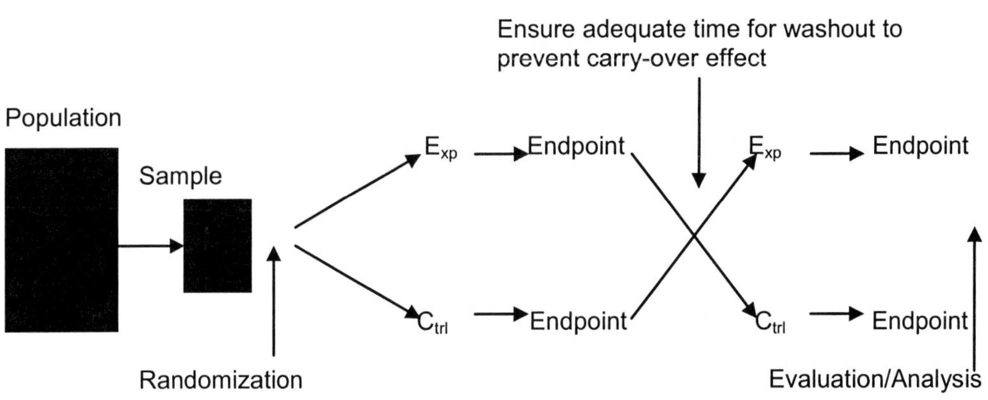

Confounding occurs when variables, other than the one(s) being studied, influence study results. Confounding variables are difficult to detect sometimes and are linked to study outcome(s) and may be linked to hypothesized cause(s). Validity of a study depends upon how well investigators minimize the influence of confounders.[9,11,15]

Example: Atherosclerosis and myocardial infarction (MI, aka heart attack): there is an association between atherosclerosis and smoking, smoking and risk for having a heart attack, and atherosclerosis and risk for having a heart attack. The proposed cause is atherosclerosis and the potential confounder is smoking.

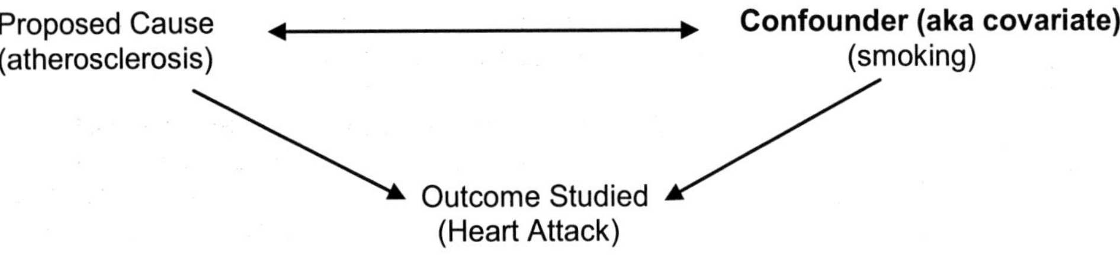

Parametric statistical methods (t-test and ANOVA) are used for analyzing normally distributed, parametric data.[4] Parametric data include interval and ratio data, but since the same parametric tests are used for both, knowing the differences between these is academic.

> Both interval and ratio scale parametric data have a predetermined order to their numbering and a consistent level of magnitude of difference between the observed data units.[1,7,8,11,12] However, for interval scale data, there is no absolute zero.[1,7,8] (e.g., Celsius or Fahrenheit) [1,8] There is an absolute zero for ratio scale data.[1,7,8] (e.g., drug concentrations, plasma glucose, FEV_1, Kelvin, heart rate, BP, # of platelets, distance, time)[1,7,8,12]

Parametric tests are more powerful than non-parametric tests.[4] Also, more information about data is generated from parametric tests.[4]

t-Test

- Student's t-test: Required assumptions: 1) normal distribution; 2) equal or nearly equal variances of the populations from which sample 1 and sample 2 were drawn.'"[4] ... While these "are important, the t-test is robust enough to be an appropriate test if an assumption is not met in the strictest sense."[4]
    - Non-paired t-test: observations between groups are independent as in a parallel study. [e.g., control vs experimental group(s) that do NOT cross-over into the alternate group(s)][4,8]

- Paired t-test (aka matched or repeated measures data): observations between groups are dependent as in a pretest/posttest study or cross-over trial. [e.g., control vs experimental group(s) that cross-over into the alternate group(s)] [4,8]

- One-tailed: Direction of difference is postulated[4]

- Two-tailed: Direction of difference is <u>not</u> postulated[4]

- **T-test is the method of choice when making a single comparison between 2 groups**.

However, when making either multiple comparisons between 2 groups or a single comparison between multiple groups, type 1 error risk increases.

- For example, when rolling dice, think of rolling ones on both dice (snake eyes) as being a type 1 error. For each roll of the dice there is a 1 in 36 chance (2.78%) of rolling snake eyes. For each statistical analysis, we generally accept a 1 in 20 chance (5%) of a type 1 error. Although the chance for snake eyes is the same for each roll and the chance for type 1 error is the same for each analysis, increasing the number of rolls and analyses increases the opportunity for snake eyes and type 1 errors, respectively.

- Said another way, the more times one rolls the dice, the more opportunity one has to roll snake eyes. It's the same with statistical testing. The more times one performs a statistical test on a particular data set, whether it be multiple comparisons of 2 groups, a single comparison of multiple groups, or multiple comparisons of multiple groups, the more likely one is to commit a type 1 error.

Example 1: A **<u>single comparison of multiple groups</u>** for which the authors and/or statisticians did not make type 1 error risk corrections.

- A trial evaluated the difference in cholesterol between pravastatin, simvastatin, atorvastatin, and rosuvastatin. First, we need to determine the number of comparisons that were made. In this example, **one endpoint (difference in cholesterol)** was evaluated for **four lipid lowering medication groups (pravastatin, simvastatin, atorvastatin, and rosuvastatin)**. For the following equations, C represents the calculated number of comparisons, X represents the number of groups being studied, and NEE represents the number of endpoints being evaluated.

  C = {[X(X-1)]/2} (NEE)

  X = 4 groups (lipid lowering medications); NEE = 1 (difference in cholesterol), so...

  C = {[4(4-1)]/2} (1)= (12/2)(1) = (6)(1) = 6 comparisons being made.

- We now need to determine the type 1 error risk if a t-test at an alpha level (α) of 0.05 were used.

  Corrected $\alpha = 1-(1-\alpha)^c = 1-(1-0.05)^6 = 0.26$

- Therefore, if the original p-value threshold of 0.05 were used, there would be a 26% chance of inappropriately rejecting the null hypothesis (type 1 error) for at least one of the 6 comparisons.[4]

Example 2: <u>Multiple comparisons of 2 groups</u> for which the authors and/or statisticians did not make type 1 error risk corrections.

- A trial evaluated chlorthalidone vs hydrochlorothiazide (HCTZ) for the primary endpoint of blood pressure (BP). In addition to this, there were other evaluated endpoints: potassium concentration (K), serum creatinine (SCr), blood urea nitrogen:serum creatinine ratio (BUN:SCr), and calcium concentration (Ca)]. First, we need to determine the number of comparisons that were made. In this example, **five endpoints (BP, K, SCr, BUN:SCr, Ca)** were evaluated for **two blood pressure medication groups (chlorthalidone and HCTZ)**. For the following equations, C represents the calculated number of comparisons, X represents the number of groups being studied, and NEE represents the number of endpoints being evaluated.

- C = {[X(X-1)]/2} (NEE)

  X = 2 groups (chlorthalidone and HCTZ); NEE = 5 (BP, K, SCr, BUN:SCr, Ca)

  C = {[2(2-1)]/2} (5) = (2/2)(5) = (1)(5) = 5 comparisons being made.

- We now need to determine the type 1 error risk if a t-test at an alpha level (α) of 0.05 were used.

  Corrected $\alpha = 1-(1-\alpha)^c = 1-(1-0.05)^5 = 0.23$

- Therefore, if the original p-value threshold of 0.05 were used, there would be a 23% chance of inappropriately rejecting the null hypothesis (type 1 error) for at least one of the 5 comparisons.[4]

Example 3: <u>Multiple comparisons of multiple groups</u> for which the authors and/or statisticians did not make type 1 error risk corrections.

- A trial evaluated metformin, glipizide, and exenatide for the primary endpoint of A1c. In addition to this, there were other evaluated endpoints: fasting blood glucose (FBG), SCr, total cholesterol (TC), low density lipoprotein cholesterol (LDL), high density lipoprotein cholesterol (HDL), and triglycerides (TG). First, we need to determine the number of comparisons that were made. In this example, **seven endpoints (A1c, FBG, SCr, TC, LDL, HDL, TG)** were evaluated for **three diabetes medication groups (metformin, glipizide, and exenatide)**. For the following equations, C represents the calculated number of comparisons, X represents the number of groups being studied, and NEE represents the number of endpoints being evaluated.

C = {[X(X-1)]/2} (NEE)

- X = 3 groups (three diabetes medications); NEE = 7 (A1c, FBG, SCr, TC, LDL, HDL, TG)

  C = {[3(3-1)]/2} (7) = (6/2)(7) = (3)(7) = 21 comparisons being made.

- We now need to determine the type 1 error risk if a t-test at an alpha level (α) of 0.05 were used.

  Corrected $\alpha = 1-(1-\alpha)^{c} = 1-(1-0.05)^{21} = 0.66$

- Therefore, if the original p-value threshold of 0.05 were used, there would be a 66% chance of inappropriately rejecting the null hypothesis (type 1 error) for at least one of the 21 comparisons.[4]

Use the above calculations to estimate type 1 error risk when investigators fail to control for multiple comparisons.

Investigators should make an effort to keep the type 1 error risk ≤ 5% (i.e., ≤0.05). The best way of doing so for multiple comparisons is by avoiding unnecessary comparisons or analyses, using the appropriate statistical test(s) for multiple comparisons, and using an alpha spending function for interim analyses. (see pages 170-171 for alpha spending function and interim analyses) However, if investigators fail to do so, there is a crude method for adjusting the preset α level based upon the number of comparisons being made: the **Bonferroni correction**. This simply divides the preset α level by the number of comparisons being made.[4] This estimates the α level that is required to reach statistical significance.[4]

Bonferroni is very conservative as the number of comparisons increases.[11] **Use the following method/calculation when investigators fail to control for multiple comparisons.**

Bonferroni correction for example 1:

$$\alpha_{adj} = \frac{\alpha_{p}}{\text{\# of comparisons}} \qquad \alpha_{adj} = \frac{0.05}{6} = 0.008$$

Based upon this Bonferroni correction, requiring the p-value to be ≤ 0.008 would ensure that type 1 error risk would not exceed 5%.[4]

Bonferroni correction for example 2:

$$\alpha_{adj} = \frac{\alpha_p}{\text{\# of comparisons}} \qquad \alpha_{adj} = \frac{0.05}{5} = 0.01$$

Based upon this Bonferroni correction, requiring the p-value to be ≤ 0.01 would ensure that type 1 error risk would not exceed 5%.[4]

Bonferroni correction for example 3:

$$\alpha_{adj} = \frac{\alpha_p}{\text{\# of comparisons}} \qquad \alpha_{adj} = \frac{0.05}{21} = 0.0024$$

Based upon this Bonferroni correction, requiring the p-value to be ≤ 0.0024 would ensure that type 1 error risk would not exceed 5%.[4]

More Bonferroni examples:

For the following equations, C represents the calculated number of comparisons, X represents the number of groups being studied, and NEE represents the number of endpoints being evaluated.

Trial evaluating 2 medications (Drug A vs Drug B) for BP control only.

2 groups, 1 endpoint evaluated

C = {[X(X-1)]/2} (NEE)
C = {[2(2-1)]/2}(1) = (2/2)(1) = (1)(1) = 1 comparison

Corrected $\alpha = 1-(1-\alpha)^c = 1-(1-0.05)^1 = 0.05$

Therefore, if the original p-value threshold of 0.05 were used, there would be a 5% chance of inappropriately rejecting the null hypothesis (type 1 error) for the 1 comparison.[4]

Bonferroni correction for an alpha of 0.05 = 0.05 ÷ 1 comparison = 0.05

Based upon this Bonferroni correction, requiring the p-value to be ≤ 0.05 would ensure that type 1 error risk would not exceed 5%.[4]

Trial evaluating 2 medications (Drug A vs Drug B) for BP and Pulse.

2 groups, 2 endpoints evaluated.

C = {[X(X-1)]/2} (NEE)
C = {[2(2-1)]/2}(2) = (2/2)(2) = (1)(2) = 2 comparisons

Corrected $\alpha = 1-(1-\alpha)^c = 1-(1-0.05)^2 = 0.0975 = 0.10$

Therefore, if the original p-value threshold of 0.05 were used, there would be a 10% chance of inappropriately rejecting the null hypothesis (type 1 error) for at least one of the 2 comparisons.[4]

Bonferroni correction for an alpha of 0.05 = 0.05 ÷ 2 comparisons = 0.025.

Based upon this Bonferroni correction, requiring the p-value to be ≤ 0.025 would ensure that type 1 error risk would not exceed 5%.[4]

Trial evaluating 2 medications (Drug A vs Drug B) for BP, Pulse, and TC.

2 groups, 3 endpoints evaluated

C = {[X(X-1)]/2} (NEE)
C = {[2(2-1)]/2}(3) = (2/2)(3) = (1)(3) = 3 comparisons

Corrected $\alpha = 1-(1-\alpha)^{c} = 1-(1-0.05)^{3} = 0.14$

Therefore, if the original p-value threshold of 0.05 were used, there would be a 14% chance of inappropriately rejecting the null hypothesis (type 1 error) for at least one of the 3 comparisons.[4]

Bonferroni correction for an alpha of 0.05 = 0.05 ÷ 3 comparisons = 0.017

Based upon this Bonferroni correction, requiring the p-value to be ≤ 0.017 would ensure that type 1 error risk would not exceed 5%.[4]

Trial evaluating 3 medications (Drugs A, B, and C) for BP control only.

3 groups, 1 endpoint evaluated

C = {[X(X-1)]/2} (NEE)
C = {[3(3-1)]/2}(1) = (6/2)(1) = (3)(1) = 3 comparisons

Corrected $\alpha = 1-(1-\alpha)^{c} = 1-(1-0.05)^{3} = 0.14$

Therefore, if the original p-value threshold of 0.05 were used, there would be a 14% chance of inappropriately rejecting the null hypothesis (type 1 error) for at least one of the 3 comparisons.[4]

Bonferroni correction for an alpha of 0.05 = 0.05 ÷ 3 comparisons = 0.017

Based upon this Bonferroni correction, requiring the p-value to be ≤ 0.017 would ensure that type 1 error risk would not exceed 5%.[4]

Trial evaluating 3 medications (Drugs A, B, and C) for BP and Pulse.

3 groups, 2 endpoints evaluated.

C = {[X(X-1)]/2} (NEE)
C = {[3(3-1)]/2}(2) = (6/2)(2) = (3)(2) = 6 comparisons

Corrected $\alpha = 1-(1-\alpha)^c = 1-(1-0.05)^6 = 0.26$

Therefore, if the original p-value threshold of 0.05 were used, there would be a 26% chance of inappropriately rejecting the null hypothesis (type 1 error) for at least one of the 6 comparisons.[4]

Bonferroni correction for an alpha of 0.05 = 0.05 ÷ 6 comparisons = 0.0083

Based upon this Bonferroni correction, requiring the p-value to be $\leq$ 0.0083 would ensure that type 1 error risk would not exceed 5%.[4]

Trial evaluating 3 medications (Drugs A, B, and C) for BP, Pulse, and TC.

3 groups, 3 endpoints evaluated

C = {[X(X-1)]/2} (NEE)
C = {[3(3-1)]/2}(3) = (6/2)(3) = (3)(3) = 9 comparisons

Corrected $\alpha = 1-(1-\alpha)^c = 1-(1-0.05)^9 = 0.37$

Therefore, if the original p-value threshold of 0.05 were used, there would be a 37% chance of inappropriately rejecting the null hypothesis (type 1 error) for at least one of the 9 comparisons.[4]

Bonferroni correction for an alpha of 0.05 = 0.05 ÷ 9 comparisons = 0.0056

Based upon this Bonferroni correction, requiring the p-value to be $\leq$ 0.0056 would ensure that type 1 error risk would not exceed 5%.[4]

Trial evaluating 4 medications (Drugs A, B, C, and D) for BP control only.

4 groups, 1 endpoint evaluated

C = {[X(X-1)]/2} (NEE)
C = {[4(4-1)]/2}(1) = (12/2)(1) = (6)(1) = 6 comparisons

Corrected $\alpha = 1-(1-\alpha)^c = 1-(1-0.05)^6 = 0.26$

Therefore, if the original p-value threshold of 0.05 were used, there would be a 26% chance of inappropriately rejecting the null hypothesis (type 1 error) for at least one of the 6 comparisons.[4]

Bonferroni correction for an alpha of 0.05 = 0.05 ÷ 6 comparisons = 0.0083

Based upon this Bonferroni correction, requiring the p-value to be ≤ 0.0083 would ensure that type 1 error risk would not exceed 5%.[4]

Trial evaluating 4 medications (Drugs A, B, C, and D) for BP and Pulse.

4 groups, 2 endpoints evaluated.

C = {[X(X-1)]/2} (NEE)
C = {[4(4-1)]/2}(2) = (12/2)(2) = (6)(2) = 12 comparisons

Corrected $\alpha = 1\text{-}(1\text{-}\ \alpha)^c = 1\text{-}(1\text{-}0.05)^{12} = 0.46$

Therefore, if the original p-value threshold of 0.05 were used, there would be a 46% chance of inappropriately rejecting the null hypothesis (type 1 error) for at least one of the 12 comparisons.[4]

Bonferroni correction for an alpha of 0.05 = 0.05 ÷ 12 comparisons = 0.0042

Based upon this Bonferroni correction, requiring the p-value to be ≤ 0.0042 would ensure that type 1 error risk would not exceed 5%.[4]

Trial evaluating 4 medications (Drugs A, B, C, and D) for BP, Pulse, and TC.

4 groups, 3 endpoints evaluated

C = {[X(X-1)]/2} (NEE)
C = {[4(4-1)]/2}(3) = (12/2)(3) = (6)(3) = 18 comparisons

Corrected $\alpha = 1\text{-}(1\text{-}\ \alpha)^c = 1\text{-}(1\text{-}0.05)^{18} = 0.60$

Therefore, if the original p-value threshold of 0.05 were used, there would be a 60% chance of inappropriately rejecting the null hypothesis (type 1 error) for at least one of the 18 comparisons.[4]

Bonferroni correction for an alpha of 0.05 = 0.05 ÷ 18 comparisons = 0.0028

Based upon this Bonferroni correction, requiring the p-value to be ≤ 0.0028 would ensure that type 1 error risk would not exceed 5%.[4]

ANOVA

A less conservative and more accepted way of minimizing type 1 error risk for multiple comparisons with parametric data is through utilization of some type of ANOVA.

ANOVA (analysis of variance) does several things.

- α level (type 1 error risk) is held constant when comparing >2 groups.[4,8]
- Tests for statistically significant difference(s) among a group's collective values.[4] In other words, intra- and inter-group variability is what is being analyzed instead of the means of the groups.[4]
- Involves calculation of an F-ratio, which answers the question, "Is 'the **variability between the groups** large enough in comparison to the **variability of data within each group** to justify the conclusion that two or more of the groups differ?'"[4,11]

  Assumptions are the same as for the t-test.[4] ANOVA is "robust enough to be an appropriate test if an assumption is not met in the strictest sense."[4] However, the more these assumptions are violated, the more likely a type 1 or 2 error will occur.

<u>ANOVAs for independent (aka non-paired) samples</u> as is the case in a parallel study. [e.g., control vs experimental group(s) that do NOT cross-over into the alternate group(s)][4,8]

One-way ANOVA is used if <u>both</u> of the following apply.[7]

- There are no identifiable confounders. The experimental groups differ in only one factor at a time (e.g., type of drug being used).
- There are ≥3 independent (aka non-paired) samples.

For example, if investigators wanted to evaluate 3 different blood pressure medications to determine which lowered blood pressure most, they could use a 1-way ANOVA as long as there were no differences between the groups that could influence the results (i.e., no confounders).

Multifactorial ANOVAs include any type of ANOVA that controls for ≥1 confounder(s) (i.e., samples differ in ≥ 2 factors).

These include:

- **Two-way ANOVA** is used if there is 1 identifiable confounder (i.e., samples differ in two factors at a time) for ≥ 2 independent (aka non-paired) samples.
    - For example, if investigators wanted to evaluate ≥ 2 weight loss products to determine which lowered weight (in total pounds) most, they could use a 2-way ANOVA as long as there was only one identifiable confounder. (e.g., heavier patients lost weight faster than less heavy patients)
- **ANACOVA, ANCOVA (analysis of covariance)** is used if there are ≥ 2 confounders and ≥ 2 independent (aka non-paired) samples.
    - **Three-way ANOVA** is used if there are 2 confounders (i.e., samples differ in three factors at a time) for ≥ 2 independent (aka non-paired) samples.
        - For example, if investigators wanted to evaluate ≥ 2 weight loss products to determine which lowered weight (in total pounds) most, they could use a 3-way ANOVA as long as there were only 2 identifiable confounders. [e.g., 1) heavier patients lose weight faster than less heavy patients and 2) differences in access to healthy foods]
    - **Four-way ANOVA** is used if there are 3 confounders (i.e., samples differ in four factors at a time) for ≥ 2 independent (aka non-paired) samples.
        - For example, if investigators wanted to evaluate ≥ 2 weight loss products to determine which lowered weight (in total pounds) most, they could use a 4-way ANOVA as long as there were only 3 identifiable confounders. [e.g., 1) heavier patients lose weight faster than less heavy patients, 2) differences in access to healthy foods, and 3) differences in access to healthy lifestyle counseling]
    - ...and so on....

ANOVAs for related (aka paired, matched, or repeated) samples as in a pretest/posttest study or cross-over trial. [e.g., control vs experimental group(s) that cross-over into the alternate group(s)] [4,8]

Repeated Measures ANOVA is used if there are no confounders and ≥ 3 related samples (aka paired). In other words, subjects would participate in more than one treatment group, as in a cross-over trial design.

For example, if investigators wanted to evaluate 3 different cholesterol lowering medications to determine which lowered cholesterol most, they could use a Repeated Measures ANOVA as long as both of the following apply:

- There are no identifiable confounders. The experimental groups differ in only one factor at a time (e.g., type of drug being used).
- Each subject serves as his/her own control. A way of doing this would be utilizing a cross-over design such that each cholesterol medication was tested in each patient with adequate washout in between treatments.

Two-way Repeated Measures ANOVA is used if there is 1 identifiable confounder and ≥ 2 related (aka paired) samples.

For example, if investigators wanted to evaluate ≥ 2 different cholesterol lowering medications to determine which lowered cholesterol most, they could use a 2-way Repeated Measures ANOVA as long as both of the following apply:

- There is only 1 identifiable confounder like differences in access to lifestyle modification counseling.
- Each subject serves as his/her own control. A way of doing this would be utilizing a cross-over design such that each cholesterol medication was tested in each patient with adequate washout in between treatments.

Repeated Measures Regression is used if there are ≥ 2 confounders and ≥ 2 related (aka paired) samples.

For example, if investigators wanted to evaluate ≥ 2 different cholesterol lowering medications to determine which lowered cholesterol most, they could use Repeated Measures Regression as long as both of the following apply:

- There are at least 2 confounders. [e.g., 1) differences in access to lifestyle modification counseling and 2) differences in access to healthier foods]

- Each subject serves as his/her own control. A way of doing this would be utilizing a cross-over design such that each cholesterol medication was tested in each patient with adequate washout in between treatments.

ANOVA will indicate if a difference exists between groups, but will not indicate where this difference exists. [11] For example, if 5 different blood pressure medications (HCTZ, chlorthalidone, lisinopril, amlodipine, and ramipril) are evaluated to determine which lowers blood pressure most, ANOVA will find if any differences exist among the collective group. However ANOVA will not indicate if the difference is between HCTZ and lisinopril, chlorthalidone and amlodipine, ramipril and amlodipine, etc. To find where the differences lie, multiple comparison methods must be performed.

Multiple Comparison Methods are types of post hoc tests that help determine which groups in a statistically significant ANOVA analysis differ. [4]

- Multiple comparison methods are ***performed only*** after ANOVA analysis produces a statistically significant F-test. Type 1 error risk will increase if one performs these post hoc tests without finding a statistically significant F-test.

- These methods are based upon the t-test but have built-in corrections to keep α level constant when >1 comparison is being made. In other words, these help control for type 1 error rate for multiple comparisons.[4]

- Examples include:

  - Least Significant Difference controls individual type 1 error rate **for each comparison.**[4]

  - Layer (aka stepwise) Methods include Newman-Keuls and Duncan. These **gradually adjust** the type 1 error rate.[4]

  - Experiment-wise Methods hold type 1 error rate constant for a set of comparisons and include:
    - Dunnett tests for contrasts with a control only.[4]
    - Dunn tests for small number of contrasts.[4]
    - Tukey tests for a large number of contrasts when ≤ 2 means are involved.[4]
    - Scheffe' tests for a large number of contrasts when >2 means are involved.[4]

	Parallel design		Crossover or pre-post design	
	2 independent samples	≥ 3 independent samples	2 related samples	≥ 3 related samples
No confounders[1]	Student's t-test (unpaired)	1-way ANOVA	Paired t-test	Repeated measures ANOVA
1 confounder[1]	2-way ANOVA	2- ANOVA	2-way repeated measures ANOVA	2-way repeated measures ANOVA
≥ 2 Confounders[1]	ANCOVA (aka ANACOVA)	ANCOVA (aka ANACOVA)	Repeated measures regression	Repeated measures regression

[1]For continuous data (interval/ratio)

Study Questions: (provided by Valerie Clinard, PharmD and Rebekah Grube, PharmD, BCPS)

(for the next 3 questions)
A study is planned to evaluate the effects of bupropion versus nicotine patches versus nicotine gum on the primary endpoint of change in the number of cigarettes smoked per day in a parallel, randomized trial. The investigators plan to include 450 subjects (150 in each arm) to reach statistical significance based upon a beta of 0.20 and alpha of 0.05.

39. Which of the following statistical tests would be the MOST appropriate? (Hint: assume no confounders)
    a. 1-way ANOVA
    b. Chi-square (χ^2)
    c. Fisher's exact
    d. Friedman
    e. Student's t-test

40. If the investigators chose to use a t-test, what would be the risk of inappropriately rejecting the null hypothesis if the original p-value threshold of 0.05 were used?
    a. 17%
    b. 14%
    c. 5%
    d. 2.5%
    e. 1.7%

41. The investigators have now decided to use Bonferroni to control for the number of comparisons in the above study. What is the adjusted alpha based upon the Bonferroni correction?
    a. 0.05
    b. 0.025
    c. 0.017
    d. 0.013
    e. 0.008

(for the next 2 questions)

42. A study is designed to evaluate the change in ejection fraction (EF) between metoprolol tartrate (Lopressor®) and metoprolol succinate (Toprol XL®). The investigators decide to perform a parallel trial in 200 patients. There were differences in baseline diet and exercise. Which of the following statistical tests would be most appropriate?
    a. One-way ANOVA
    b. Chi-square (χ^2)
    c. McNemar χ^2
    d. ANCOVA (aka ANACOVA)
    e. Students t-test

43. The investigators decide to change the trial design from the above question to a cross-over trial so that confounding by diet and exercise would be minimized. Which statistical test would now be most appropriate?
    a. Wilcoxon Signed Rank
    b. Paired t-test
    c. Repeated measures regression
    d. 2-way repeated measures ANOVA
    e. ANCOVA

44. Which of the following is a required assumption for the t-Test?
    a. The total population (N) should be < 40.
    b. Data should be normally distributed.
    c. At least 1 confounder must be identified.
    d. Observations within each sample must be dependent (as in paired data/cross-over design).

(For the next 3 questions)

45. A multi-center, double blind, parallel study is being conducted to evaluate the efficacy of Drug X, Drug Y, and Drug Z in improving LDL, HDL, and TG. (Assume a pre-set alpha of 0.05 and beta of 0.20). Which of the following statistical tests would be the MOST appropriate? (Hint: assume no confounders)
    a. 1-way ANOVA
    b. Chi-square (χ^2)
    c. 2-way ANOVA
    d. ANCOVA
    e. Student's t-test

46. If the investigators chose to use a t-test, what would be the risk of inappropriately rejecting the null hypothesis if the original p-value threshold of 0.05 were used?
    a. 17%
    b. 14%
    c. 5%
    d. 26%
    e. 37%

47. To reduce the risk for a Type 1 error, and control for the number of comparisons, a Bonferroni t-Test is performed. What is the adjusted level of statistical significance based upon the Bonferroni correction?
    a. $p \leq 0.05$
    b. $p \leq 0.008$
    c. $p \leq 0.017$
    d. $p \leq 0.0056$

(For the next 2 questions)

48. A study is being designed to evaluate change in blood pressure between Camelpril and Valpril. The investigators decide to conduct a trial in 2000 patients. A total of 1000 patients will be randomized to receive Camelpril and 1000 patients will be randomized to receive Valpril for 24 weeks. After a 2-week washout, subjects will receive the other agent. Which statistical test would be MOST appropriate for this study? (Assume no confounders identified)
    a. Paired t-Test
    b. Non-paired t-Test
    c. Repeated measures ANOVA
    d. 2-way repeated measures ANOVA
    e. Repeated measures regression

49. If two confounders were identified, which statistical test would be MOST appropriate?
    a. Paired t-Test
    b. 3-way ANOVA
    c. Repeated Measures Regression
    d. Repeated measures ANOVA
    e. 2-way repeated measures ANOVA

Answers to Study Questions:

39. a - Change in the number of cigarettes smoked per is parametric data since it is scored on a continuum and there is a consistent level of magnitude of difference between data units. Since there are 3 groups being evaluated, and no identified confounders, a 1-way ANOVA is appropriate. Since this will be a parallel trial, if there were only 2 groups and no identified confounders, a t-test would be appropriate. Chi-square and Fisher's exact are for nominal data. Friedman is for ordinal data.

40. b

3 groups (bupropion, nicotine patches, nicotine gum)
1 endpoint evaluated (change in the number of cigarettes smoked)

For the following calculations, C represents the calculated number of comparisons, X represents the number of groups being studied, and NEE represents the number of endpoints being evaluated.

C = {[X(X-1)]/2} (NEE)
C = {[3(3-1)]/2}(1) = (6/2)(1) = (3)(1) = 3 comparisons

Corrected $\alpha = 1-(1-\alpha)^c = 1-(1-0.05)^3 = 0.14$

Therefore, if the original p-value threshold of 0.05 were used, there would be a 14% chance of inappropriately rejecting the null hypothesis (type 1 error) for at least one of the 3 comparisons.

41. c

3 groups (bupropion, nicotine patches, nicotine gum)
1 endpoint evaluated (change in the number of cigarettes smoked)

For the following calculations, C represents the calculated number of comparisons, X represents the number of groups being studied, and NEE represents the number of endpoints being evaluated.

C = {[X(X-1)]/2} (NEE)
C = {[3(3-1)]/2}(1) = (6/2)(1) = (3)(1) = 3 comparisons

Bonferroni correction for an alpha of 0.05 = 0.05 ÷ 3 comparisons = 0.017

Based upon this Bonferroni correction, requiring the p-value to be ≤ 0.017 would ensure that type 1 error risk would not exceed 5%.

42. d - Change in EF is parametric data since it is scored on a continuum and there is a consistent level of magnitude of difference between data units. Since there are 2 confounders (diet and exercise) in this parallel trial, a 3-way ANOVA needs to be used to control for these. Three-way, 4-way, 5-way, etc. ANOVAs are also known as ANACOVA or ANCOVA, so answer "d" is correct, ANCOVA. Since only two groups are being evaluated in this parallel trial, if there were no confounders, a t-test would be most appropriate. Chi-square is for nominal data. One-way ANOVA is useful in analyzing parametric data if there were at least 3 groups and no confounders.

43. b - Change in EF is parametric data since it is scored on a continuum and there is a consistent level of magnitude of difference between data units. Since there are 2 groups being evaluated and no confounders in this cross-over design, a paired t-test is most appropriate. If there were 1 confounder, a 2-way repeated measures ANOVA would be most appropriate. If there were 2 or more confounders, repeated measures regression would be most appropriate.

44. b

45. a - Changes in LDL, HDL, and TG are all parametric data since they are scored on a continuum and there is a consistent level of magnitude of difference between data units. Since there are 3 groups and no identifiable confounders in this parallel trial, a 1-way ANOVA is appropriate. Two-way ANOVA would be useful if there were 1 confounder. ANCOVA would be useful if there were at least 2 confounders. If there were only 2 groups and no identifiable confounders, a t-test would be appropriate. Chi-square is used for nominal data.

46. e

3 groups (drug X, drug Y, drug Z), 3 endpoints evaluated (LDL, HDL, TG)

For the following calculations, C represents the calculated number of comparisons, X represents the number of groups being studied, and NEE represents the number of endpoints being evaluated.

C = {[X(X-1)]/2} (NEE)
C = {[3(3-1)]/2}(3) = (6/2)(3) = (3)(3) = 9 comparisons

Corrected $\alpha = 1-(1-\alpha)^{c} = 1-(1-0.05)^{9} = 0.37$

Therefore, if the original p-value threshold of 0.05 were used, there would be a 37% chance of inappropriately rejecting the null hypothesis (type 1 error) for at least one of the 9 comparisons.

47. d

3 groups (drug X, drug Y, drug Z), 3 endpoints evaluated (LDL, HDL, TG)

For the following calculations, C represents the calculated number of comparisons, X represents the number of groups being studied, and NEE represents the number of endpoints being evaluated.

C = {[X(X-1)]/2} (NEE)
C = {[3(3-1)]/2}(3) = (6/2)(3) = (3)(3) = 9 comparisons

Bonferroni correction for an alpha of 0.05 = 0.05 ÷ 9 comparisons = 0.0056

Based upon this Bonferroni correction, requiring the p-value to be ≤ 0.0056 would ensure that type 1 error risk would not exceed 5%.

48. a - Change in BP is parametric data since it is scored on a continuum and there is a consistent level of magnitude of difference between data units. Since patients will serve as their own controls by crossing over from receiving one medication into receiving the other medication, this is a cross-over trial design.

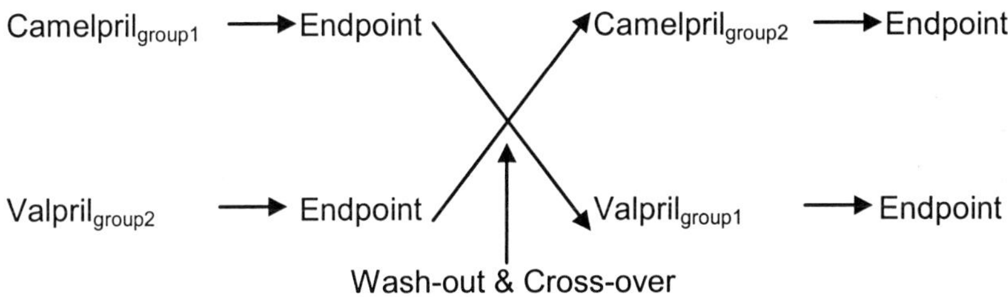

Group 1 will receive Camelpril during the first part of the crossover trial, then Group 1 will receive Valpril for the second part of the trial.

Group 2 will receive Valpril during the first part of the crossover trial, then Group 2 will receive Camelpril for the second part of the trial.

Since there are 2 groups being evaluated and no confounders in this cross-over design, a paired t-test is most appropriate. If this were a parallel design, a non-paired t-test would be most appropriate. If there were 1 confounder, a 2-way repeated measures ANOVA would be most appropriate. If there were 2 or more confounders, repeated measures regression would be most appropriate. If there were 3 related groups and no confounders, repeated measures ANOVA would be most appropriate.

49. c - Since there are 2 groups being evaluated and 2 confounders in this cross-over design, a repeated measures regression is most appropriate. Repeated measures regression would also be appropriate if more than 2 confounders were identified. If there were only 1 confounder, a 2-way repeated measures ANOVA would be most appropriate. If there were 3 related groups and no confounders, repeated measures ANOVA would be most appropriate.

Part 5: Statistical Inference Techniques for Hypothesis Testing with Nonparametric Data[5]

Nonparametric statistical methods are used for analyzing data that are not normally distributed and cannot be defined as interval or ratio data.[5] This chapter will start with statistical tests for nominal data, followed by tests for ordinal data. As noted in part 1 of this text, with nominal data, numbers are purely arbitrary. There is no order of ranking of severity. Nominal data may be dichotomous or categorical.

- Dichotomous (binary): lived/died, yes/no, hospitalized/not hospitalized.[11,12]
- Categorical: There is no order or inherent value for nominal categorical data. (e.g., race, eye color, hair color, religion, blood type, ARF/HF/DM)[11,12]

Nonparametric Tests for Nominal Data

The most common tests for proportions and frequencies of nominal data include chi-square (χ^2) and fisher's exact.

Chi-Square (χ^2) tests are "used to answer questions about **rates, proportions, or frequencies**" when sample size (N) is >20.[5,11]

For matrices that are larger than 2x2, χ^2 tests will detect difference(s) between groups, but will not indicate where the difference(s) lie(s).[5,11] To find this, post-hoc tests are needed.[11] These post-hoc tests should only be performed if the χ^2 test was statistically significant. Doing otherwise will increase type 1 error risk.

As noted in this chapter, depending upon a given study's design, there are several types of χ^2 tests that can be used.

Assumptions must be met if χ^2 is to be properly applied.[5]

- **Only nominal data may be analyzed.** These may include ordinal or parametric data that have been degraded to nominal data.[5] However, it should be noted that degrading parametric data into non-parametric data, or degrading ordinal data into nominal data, is generally discouraged since doing so usually decreases power to detect meaningful differences.[32]
    - Ordinal data degradation example: changing from a 10 point pain scale to whether or not pain is present.
    - Parametric degradation example: changing from differences in blood pressure in terms of mmHg to whether or not hypertension is present.

- **There must be a logical reason for nominal group classifications.**[5]

- **No cells in a 2x2 matrix can have a frequency of <5. For 2x2 matrix**, see Fisher's exact test.[5]

- **For matrices that are larger than 2x2, no cell can have a value of zero and no more than 20% of cells can have a frequency of <5.** In either of these cases, there are two possible solutions: either 1) data can be combined in a logical manner or 2) more data must be collected.[5] If categories are combined, there must be a rationale other than solely being for convenience's sake.[5]

Although rarely used, Yates Correction for Continuity helps decrease type 1 error risk in 2x2 matrices.[5] Yates is not needed in 3 cases: if the χ^2 matrix is larger than 2x2, N>40, or if χ^2 does not reach statistical significance (because it is impossible to make a type 1 error if no statistically significant difference is detected).[5]

An example of when a χ^2 test might be useful would be if four medications, chlorthalidone, lisinopril, amlodipine, and atenolol, were evaluated for 5 years to determine any differences in death rate.

Medication	Lived	Died
Chlorthalidone	190	5
Lisinopril	220	6
Amlodipine	230	6
Atenolol	225	10

This kind of table is sometimes referred to as a **contingency table**. It expresses the idea that one variable (living vs dying) may be contingent upon another variable (medication used). There are 4 medications and 2 possible results (living vs dying), so this is called a 4x2 table or matrix.

Types of χ^2 tests

- χ^2 Test of Independence (aka test of association) is used to compare ≥ 2 independent (aka non-paired) samples. (≥ 2x2 table, i.e., 2x2, 2x3, 4, 5, 3x3, etc.).[5,8,11]

- χ^2 Goodness of Fit is used to compare sample group data with known or estimated population data.[5] (N must be >20, 2x2 matrix or larger)[5]
  - An example of when this may be useful is evaluating a new immunoassay's ability to accurately detect presence of an infection relative to a gold standard test.

- McNemar χ^2 is used for paired data, but is limited to a single comparison between 2 groups.[8,17] (i.e., 2x2 table)

- It is the nominal level analogue of the paired t-test.
- There are many variations of statistical tests like McNemar. Think of McNemar variations for studies with a paired design. (i.e., repeated, matched data, cross-over, pre-test/post-test)
- An example of when this may be useful is evaluating attainment of goal blood pressure (i.e., either achieving or not achieving goal BP) with chlorthalidone versus lisinopril in a cross-over trial.

- Mantel-Haenszel χ^2 is used if there is 1 identifiable confounder and only 2 independent (aka non-paired) samples.[8,17,19]
  - It is the nominal level analogue of the 2-way ANOVA.
  - As is discussed later, Mantel-Haenszel is also used many times in meta-analyses to pool odds ratios from different studies.
  - There are many variations of statistical tests like Mantel-Haenszel. Think of Mantel-Haenszel variations when there is a need to control for one confounder with 2 independent (aka, non-paired, parallel designed) groups.
  - An example of when this may be useful is evaluating HF exacerbations (i.e., either having or not having a HF exacerbation) with chlorthalidone versus lisinopril in a parallel trial when there is a confounder of average baseline blood pressures being different.

- Log-Linear Analysis (χ^2 type, aka Logistic Regression)[19]: Used for ≥2 confounders and >2 variables. (i.e., ≥ 3x3 table) [19]
  - Similar to a multiple regression type of data analysis. Calculates a χ^2 at each stage of analysis. Nominal level analogue of the ANCOVA (ANACOVA) that was discussed earlier.
  - An example of when this may be useful is evaluating HF exacerbations (i.e., either having or not having a HF exacerbation) with chlorthalidone versus lisinopril versus amlodipine when there are 2 confounders of average baseline blood pressures and LDL-cholesterol being different among the 3 groups.

Fisher's Exact test - Assumptions are the same as for χ^2 tests, but this is <u>not</u> a type of χ^2 test.[5]

- As with χ^2, only nominal data may be analyzed. These may include ordinal or parametric data that have been degraded to nominal data.[5] However, it should be noted that degrading parametric data into non-parametric data, or degrading ordinal data into nominal data, is generally discouraged since doing so usually decreases power to detect meaningful differences.[32]
- Used in a 2x2 matrix when N ≤ 20. [5,8]
- Also used when N = 20-40 and the number of individuals in **one** cell of a 2x2 matrix is <5. [5]
- May be used for paired and non-paired data. (i.e., parallel and cross-over trials or pre-post test comparisons)

(modification of Figure 4, page 1057)[5a]

Type of Data	N	Other Comments	Proper Test
Nominal, or other that has been **transformed to nominal**	Must be > 20	≥ 2 x 2 matrix (i.e. 2x3, 4, 5, etc. or 3x3); No cell of a 2x2 matrix, or **more** than 20% of the cells of a larger matrices, may have a frequency of less than 5. Comparison of **≥ 2 groups** or types of outcomes	χ^2 test of independence (aka χ^2 test of association)
	Must be > 20	≥ 2 x 2 matrix (i.e. 2x3, 4, 5, etc. or 3x3); No cell of a 2x2 matrix, or **more** than 20% of the cells of a larger matrices, may have a frequency of less than 5. Comparison **of one experimental group to a previously defined population**	χ^2 goodness of fit test
(If the cell frequency is < 5 for two or more of the cells, then it is **controversial** whether Fisher's exact should be calculated.)[18]	≤ 20	2 x 2 matrix only	Fisher's exact test
	> 20, but < 40 What if >40? Controversial[18]	2 x 2 matrix only; used when cell frequency is less than 5 for one of the cells	Fisher's exact test

Nonparametric Rank Tests for Ordinal Data

Ordinal data are categorical, but scored on a continuum, *without* a consistent level of magnitude of difference between ranks[1,7,8,11,12] Some examples include pain scale, NYHA class, heart failure stage, trauma score, Glasgow Coma Score, Likert-like scales- poor/fair/good/very good/excellent, and cancer staging.[1,8,11,12,15,27]

With the following tests, only ordinal data may be analyzed. This may include parametric data that have been degraded to ordinal data.[5] However, it should be noted that degrading parametric data into ordinal data is generally discouraged since doing so usually decreases power to detect meaningful differences.[32]

- **Mann-Whitney U Test** and **Wilcoxon Rank Sum** are used when 1 comparison is being made with 2 independent (i.e., non-paired) groups.[5,11] These are non-parametric analogues of the non-paired student's t-test and are **appropriate when data are <u>not</u> grouped or lumped together for further analysis.**[5,8]
  - An example of when this may be useful is evaluating any difference in NYHA class with metoprolol versus carvedilol in a parallel trial.

- **Kolmogorov-Smirnov** Test is also used when 1 comparison is being made with 2 independent (i.e., non-paired) groups and is a non-parametric analog of the non-paired student's t-test just as with Mann-Whitney U and Wilcoxon Rank Sum. However, Kolmogorov-Smirnov is **appropriate when data are grouped or lumped together for further analysis.**
  - An example of when this may be useful is evaluating any difference in Glasgow Coma Score (and subsequently calculating and evaluating any difference in Trauma Score) when evaluating two different treatment algorithms for emergency department trauma patients in a parallel trial. [5]

- **Wilcoxon Signed Rank** (NOT to be confused with wilcoxon rank sum) is used when 1 comparison is being made with 2 related (i.e., paired) groups and is a non-parametric analog of the **paired** t-test.[5,8] It can be used when parametric data are not normally distributed.[5]
  - An example of when this may be useful is evaluating any difference in chronic osteoarthritis pain (not acute pain) via a 10-point scale with acetaminophen versus tramadol in a cross-over trial.

- **Kruskal-Wallis** is used when at least 2 comparisons are made with at least 3 independent (i.e., non-paired) groups. Depending upon the number of comparisons being made, it serves as the non-parametric analog of one-way or multifactorial ANOVAs.[5,8]
  - An example of when this may be useful is evaluating any difference in NYHA class with metoprolol versus carvedilol versus bisoprolol in a parallel trial.

- **Friedman** is used when at least 2 comparisons are made with at least 3 related (i.e., paired) groups. Depending upon the number of comparisons being made, it serves as the non-parametric analog of repeated measures ANOVA, two way repeated measures ANOVA or repeated measures regression.[5,8]
  - An example of when this may be useful is evaluating any difference in chronic osteoarthritis pain (not acute pain) via a 10-point scale with acetaminophen versus tramadol versus opioid analgesia in a cross-over trial.

As with χ^2 and ANOVA tests for >2 groups, Kruskal-Wallis and Friedman will detect difference(s) between groups, but will not indicate where difference(s) lie(s).[11] To find this, post-hoc tests are needed.[11] These post-hoc tests should only be performed if Kruskal-Wallis or Friedman was statistically significant. Doing otherwise will increase type 1 error risk.

There are a couple of tests that can help control for confounders with ordinal data. ANOVA Rank Tests can be used to account for confounders with an independent (i.e., non-paired), ordinal data set. Repeated Measures Regression can be used to account for confounders with a dependent (i.e., paired), ordinal data set.

(modification of Table, page 1058)[5b] Type of Data	# of Groups Compared	# of Comparisons	Do Subjects "Serve as their own controls"?	Test
Ordinal: or interval/ratio data that does not meet parametric test assumptions. **Not grouped** into cumulative frequency distribution. (i.e. individual scores or data values are **not lumped** together into groups for further analysis)	2	1	No	Mann-Whitney U Wilcoxon Rank Sum (non-parametric analogues of the non-paired t-test)
Ordinal: or interval/ratio data that does not meet parametric test assumptions. **Grouped** into a cumulative frequency distribution. (i.e., individual scores or data values **are lumped** together into groups for further analysis)	2	1	No	Kolmogorov-Smirnov (also a non-parametric analog of the non-paired t-test)
Ordinal: or interval/ratio data that does not meet parametric test assumptions.	2	1	Yes	Wilcoxon Signed Rank (non-parametric analog of the paired t-test)
Ordinal: or interval/ratio data that does not meet parametric test assumptions.	≥ 3	≥ 2	No	Kruskal-Wallis (non-parametric analog of one-way or multifactorial ANOVA depending on the # of comparisons being made)
Ordinal: or interval/ratio data that does not meet parametric test assumptions.	≥ 3	≥ 2	Yes	Friedman (non-parametric analog of the repeated measures ANOVA, two way repeated measures ANOVA or repeated measures regression depending on the # of comparisons being made.)

Study Questions: (provided by Valerie Clinard, PharmD and Rebekah Grube, PharmD, BCPS)

(for the next 2 questions)
The makers of eplerenone want to design a study to compare their medication to the current standard of spironolactone in the treatment of heart failure. They decide to perform a parallel trial of the two agents in 2000 patients with NYHA class III/IV heart failure over 1 year. The primary endpoint is change in NYHA class score.

50. Based upon the above study, which statistical test would be most appropriate to analyze the outcome data? (Hint: assume no confounders)
    a. McNemar χ^2
    b. Friedman
    c. Chi-square(χ^2)
    d. Mann-Whitney U
    e. Student's t-test

51. The investigators decide that a better outcome would be mortality, instead of change in NYHA class score, and change their primary endpoint accordingly. Which of the following statistical tests would now be the most appropriate? (Hint: assume no confounders)
    a. McNemar χ^2
    b. Friedman
    c. Chi-square (χ^2)
    d. Mann-Whitney U
    e. Student's t-test

52. A randomized, parallel trial is being designed to evaluate all-cause mortality with Drug X and Drug Y. Approximately 5000 patients will be enrolled in the study. What type of statistical test would be MOST appropriate (assume no confounders)?
    a. ANACOVA
    b. Mann Whitney U
    c. Chi-square
    d. Fisher's Exact

(for the next 2 questions)
A randomized, parallel trial is being designed to evaluate the efficacy of Drug T, Drug V and Drug Z in 800 heart failure patients. NYHA Class will be utilized as the primary endpoint.

53. What type of statistical test would be MOST appropriate? (assume no confounders)
    a. Student's t-Test
    b. ANACOVA
    c. Mann Whitney U
    d. Dunn Test
    e. Kruskal-Wallis

54. What if this were a cross-over trial?
    a. Fisher's Exact
    b. Wilcoxon Rank Sum
    c. Wilcoxon Signed Rank
    d. Kruskal-Wallis
    e. Friedman

Answers to Study Questions:

50. d - Change in NYHA classification is ordinal data (scored on a continuum, without a consistent level of magnitude of difference between ranks). There is one comparison (change in NYHA class) being made between two groups (new medication vs spironolactone), so either a Mann-Whitney U or Wilcoxon Rank Sum can be used. Friedman is also used for ordinal data, but is used when there are at least 3 groups at least 2 comparisons being made. Chi-square is used for nominal data. T-test is used for parametric data.

51. c - Mortality is nominal data. Also there are 2000 patients being evaluated. Therefore chi-square should be used. McNemar chi-square is utilized for paired data as would be the case in a cross-over or pre-test vs post-test study. Mann-Whitney U and Friedman are used for ordinal data analysis. T-test is used for parametric data analysis.

52. c - Mortality is nominal data. Also there are 5000 patients being evaluated. Therefore chi-square should be used. Fisher's Exact should not be used if more than 20 patients (some say more than 40) were being evaluated. Mann-Whitney U is used for ordinal data analysis. ANACOVA is used for parametric data analysis.

53. e - NYHA classification is ordinal data (scored on a continuum, without a consistent level of magnitude of difference between ranks). Three groups are being compared: Drug T, Drug V, Drug Z. Multiple comparisons are being made. In this case three comparisons are being made with regard to NYHA class: Drug T vs Drug V, Drug V vs Drug Z, and Drug T vs Drug Z. Also this is a parallel trial. Therefore Kruskal-Wallis should be used. Mann-Whitney U is used for ordinal data when there is one comparison of two groups in a parallel design. T-test and ANACOVA are used for parametric data. Dunn is a post-hoc test performed after a significant ANOVA (or ANCOVA, ANACOVA) to determine where the difference(s) exist.

54. e - If this were a cross-over study, Friedman would be appropriate. Wilcoxon Rank Sum is used for ordinal data when there is one comparison of two groups in a parallel design. Wilcoxon Signed Rank is used for ordinal data when there is one comparison of two groups and patients serve as their own controls as would be the case for a cross-over or pre-test vs post-test design. Kruskal-Wallis is used if there are at least two comparisons of at least three groups in a parallel design. Fisher's Exact is used for nominal data.

Part 6: Correlation and Regression[6]

Correlation simply explains the strength of a relationship between 2 variables.[6,8,32] These do not need to be independent variables. They can be solely dependent variables.[32]

Remember that an independent variable is "the intervention or what is being manipulated" in a study. (e.g., a drug being evaluated).[15] A dependent variable is the outcome of interest within a study."[15] (aka endpoint of the study; e.g., hospitalization, death, BP, cholesterol).

Population correlation coefficient (rho)[6] When more than 2 variables are used, a **multiple correlation coefficient (R)** is calculated.

Sample correlation coefficient for ordinal data: **Spearman's rho or Spearman's rank order r**.[6,11]

Only **ordinal** data may be analyzed with Spearman. These may include parametric data that have been degraded to ordinal data.[5] However, it should be noted that degrading parametric data into ordinal data is generally discouraged since doing so usually decreases power to detect meaningful differences.[32]

- Parametric degradation example: changing from differences in blood pressure in terms of mmHg to stages of hypertension (no hypertension, pre-hypertension, stage 1 hypertension, stage 2 hypertension).

Spearman is "based upon the rank order of the individual data points and not the actual numerical values."[6]

Sample correlation coefficient for continuous (i.e., parametric) data: **Pearson correlation coefficient or Pearson product-moment r**.[6,11] Pearson quantifies strength of the linear relationship between 2 continuous (parametric) variables.[6,11]

Regardless of the type of correlation used (Spearman or Pearson)...

- r ranges from $^{-}1$ to $^{+}1$.[6,11]
- $^{-}1$ = perfect negative linear relationship.[6,11]
- $^{+}1$ = perfect positive linear relationship.[6,11]
- Zero = no relationship.[6,11]
- H_o is that r = zero (i.e., no relationship between variables).[6] So, "the closer r is to zero, allegedly the weaker the relationship."[6,11]

- A "small correlation between 2 variables can be due to:

    1. little association between 2 variables or…

    2. large errors in the measurement of the variables."[6]

- There is not a consistent level of magnitude of difference between r values.[32] Therefore, r of 0.25 is **not** half the relationship of an r of 0.5 and "an r of ± 0.5 does **not** imply that the strength of the relationship is 'half-way' between no correlation/relationship and a perfect correlation."[6,32]

- The strength of a relationship is dependent upon the data being evaluated. In one field of study an r of 0.6 may be a strong correlation, whereas in another field of study an r of 0.9 may be required to indicate a strong correlation.

- Some general guidelines are:

    - $r < 0.25$: "doubtful" correlation[32,33]

    - $r = 0.26 - 0.5$: "fair" correlation[32,33]

    - $r = 0.51 - 0.75$: "good" correlation[32,33]

    - $r > 0.75$: "superior" correlation[32,33]

- r-value confidence intervals can be calculated.[11]

    - e.g., $r = 0.74$ (95%CI: 0.53 - 0.98)

Pay more attention to the r-value than the p-value.[8] A lower p-value does not imply greater correlation. It only means that "chance" is less likely to explain any observed correlation.[6,8,17]

Most of the time, **relationships are "confounded by extraneous variables."**[6] For example, temperature increases the closer one moves towards the equator, but altitude and weather patterns are confounders that prevent a perfect relationship.[6] As seen in this example, the direction of a relationship may be easy to predict, however the strength of that relationship is not.[6.32] Correlation helps explain this.[6,8,32]

The same happens with patients, meds, and diseases. For example, there is an association with overuse of albuterol and mortality. But there are multiple confounders that prevent an absolute understanding of this relationship. These confounders include the type of controller medication being used, inhalation technique, medication adherence, concomitant disease states (COPD, HF), concomitant medications (beta-blockers), various triggers (air pollution, pets, mold, and cockroach exposure), etc.

Correlation has many limitations. Although it does a good job of recognizing and measuring the strength of relationship(s) between variables, detecting a correlation does not establish causality.[6,32] Remember the ageless question of which came first, the chicken or the egg? More relevant examples include:

- Which came first? Does overuse of albuterol lead to poorly responsive, severe asthma attacks? ... or does poorly responsive, severe asthma lead to albuterol overuse?
- Which came first, renal dysfunction or hypertension? Are there other factors that influence this relationship? Correlation does not help us establish whether renal dysfunction causes hypertension or hypertension causes renal dysfunction.
- Additionally, correlations do not have the ability to predict 1 variable based upon another. Regression analysis is required to predict 1 variable based upon one or more other variables.

Simple Linear Regression takes correlation 1 step further. It not only recognizes and measures the strength of relationship(s) between variables, it also describes a relationship such that one is able to develop an equation for predicting 1 variable (dependent variable) from 1 other variable (independent variable).[6,8]

- Unlike correlation, regression analysis requires at least 1 independent (or predictor) variable. The independent variable(s) is/are used to predict a dependent variable.[6,8,32] For example, a person's renal function as determined by creatinine clearance (dependent variable) may be predicted by blood pressure (independent variable). The higher a person's blood pressure, the more likely the patient's renal function (serum creatinine - SCr) will worsen. Renal function (SCr) is the dependent variable because it "depends upon" a person's blood pressure.
- As with correlation, pay more attention to the r-value than the p-value.[8] A lower p-value does not imply a stronger relationship is present. It only means that "chance" is less likely to explain any observed relationship.[6,8,17]
  - Regression defines the line of best fit where m = slope of the line, y is the dependent variable, x is the independent variable, and b is the y-intercept of the line.[6]
  - $y = mx + b$

- The regression line of best fit is calculated by the "least-squares method" which calculates the line that is nearest to running through all data points with the least amount of error.[6] This line of best fit should **not** be extrapolated beyond the data points of either extreme because what will happen to the relationship beyond these extremes is unknown.[32]

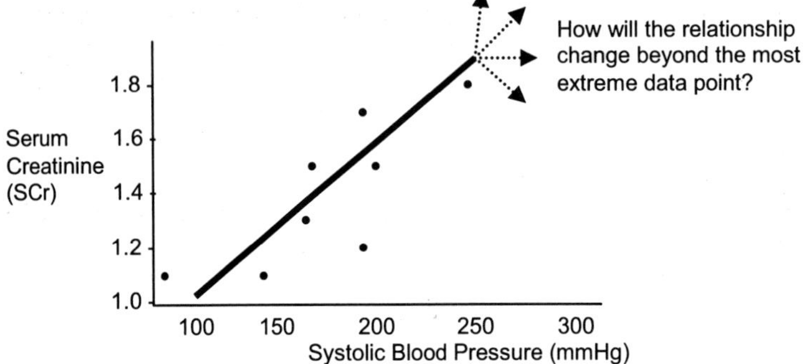

- "The closer the absolute value of r is to ± 1, the closer the predicted value(s) of y will lie to the regression line."[6] The closer the predicted value(s) lie(s) to the regression line, the less the error of prediction of the dependent variable based upon the independent variable(s).

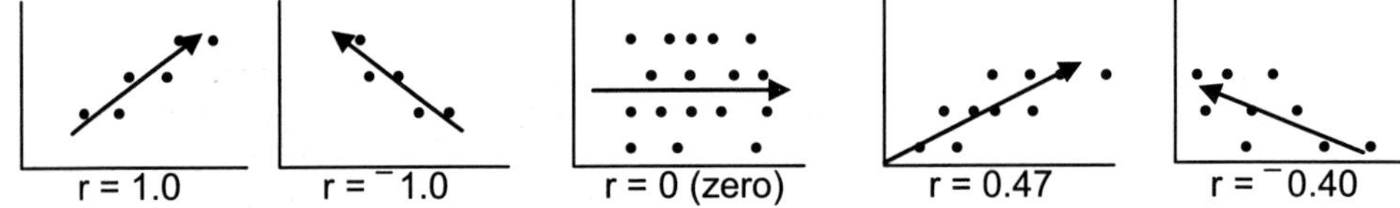

- r is tested to see if the slope of the line is different from zero (zero = no relationship). Confidence intervals (95% CI) can be calculated. If α is 0.05 and the 95% CI includes zero, then the null hypothesis (H_o) cannot be rejected.[32]

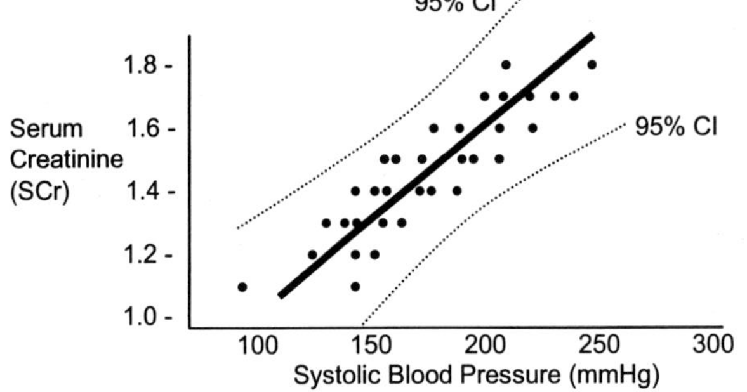

The 95% CI tails off Near the extreme values where less data have been collected.

Coefficient of Determination

r-squared (r^2) is known as the coefficient of determination. It "represents the percentage of variation in y (dependent variable) that is accounted for by x (independent variable)."[27] So if r = 0.94, then r^2 (r-squared) = 0.88 and this indicates that 88% of variation in y is explained by x.[6] For example, a study produces a correlation/regression analysis between renal function (creatinine clearance – CrCl) and hypertension reporting an r = 0.6. Therefore $r^2 = 0.6^2 = 0.36$ and one could say that 36% of renal function (CrCl) may be explained by blood pressure.

- Conversely, $1\text{-}r^2$ represents the proportion of the variation that is **not** related to the independent variable(s). So if $r^2 = 0.36$, then $1\text{-}r^2 = 0.64$ and one could say that 64% of renal function (CrCl) is **not** explained by blood pressure.
    - This residual variation is sometimes referred to as the **coefficient of non-determination**.[6,32]

Multiple Regression

When there is one independent variable, a **simple linear regression** may be performed. However when ≥ 2 independent variables are used to predict a dependent variable, **multiple (or multivariate) regression analysis (MRA)** is utilized.[8,32]

- Most diseases are dependent upon multiple risk factors (i.e., multiple independent variables). Therefore, MRA is generally required to help predict disease risk (dependent variable) in the medical literature. For example, the national cholesterol guidelines utilize multiple regression to help establish atherosclerotic cardiovascular disease (ASCVD) risk for patients based upon population data. A patient's ASCVD risk is the dependent variable because its estimate "depends upon" several independent variables. The independent variables include gender, race, age, total cholesterol, HDL-cholesterol, smoking status, systolic blood pressure, whether or not a patient is being treated for hypertension, or has diabetes. All of these independent variables are used to help predict a patient's ASCVD risk.

- MRA "produces many 'r' values, each of which is compared to 'r' values from other models."[8]

- **Multiple Linear Regression** is used with **parametric (aka continuous)** outcomes like BP and lipid values.[35]

- "**Logistic Regression** is used with **dichotomous** outcomes" like death and hospitalization.[27,35] Converting these variables to log scale helps change non-normally distributed data to a normal distribution.[11]

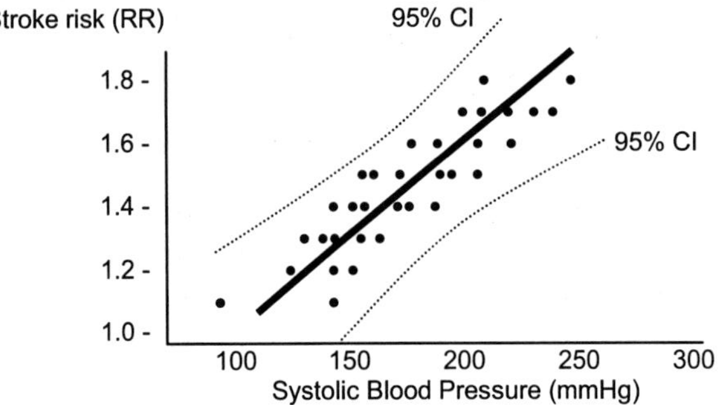

- **Cox Proportional Hazards Regression** is "used when the outcome is the length of time" it takes to have an event.[35] For example, Cox would be appropriate when evaluating time until death or hospitalization for two different heart failure treatments like spironolactone vs placebo.[11,35] This is a type of survival analysis that is useful for "longitudinal studies in which persons may be lost to follow-up."[35]

  - Cox Proportion Hazards **assumes** the "differences between groups are constant" over the entire time of the study.[16] This is called the **proportionality assumption** and is generally a faulty assumption given the nature of clinical events. For example, for some surgeries, mortality is higher during the immediate post-op period relative to 1 year post surgery.

  - Fortunately, Cox Proportional Hazards Regression Analysis can utilize **time-varying covariates** whose values are able to change over time such that the "model **can correctly account for HRs that vary over the course of a study**."[35]

In studies, authors may actually calculate and report both correlation and regression analyses. This is because correlation can help "support the interpretation" of the regression analysis.[32]

The existence of a statistical association with correlation or regression analysis is **not** in itself evidence of causality. In the examples described in this chapter, each of the variables (asthma exacerbation vs albuterol overuse, hypertension vs renal dysfunction) could cause the other. Additionally, the variables could be affected by other influences (aka confounding variables). So to explain causality, considerations such as the type of analysis being performed must be addressed. (i.e., case-control vs cohort vs RCT)

To emphasize this point, an "r = 0.99 does not imply causation any more than an r = 0.85."[6] However, correlation and regression analysis may stimulate future research with stronger methodology (e.g., RCTs) which can help establish causation.[6,32]

Study Questions:

A retrospective study produces correlation/regression analysis between a high sodium intake (>2.4 grams/day) and hypertension reporting an $r = 0.65$.

55. Which of the following is correct?
    a. 42% of HTN is caused by high sodium intake
    b. 58% of HTN is not explained by high sodium intake
    c. 58% of HTN is not caused by high sodium intake
    d. 35% of HTN is not explained by high sodium intake
    e. 65% of HTN may be explained by high sodium intake

56. No correlation would be denoted by...
    a. $r = 0$
    b. $r = 1$
    c. $r = {}^{-}1$
    d. $r = 0.5$
    e. $r = {}^{-}0.5$

57. Which of the following statements is TRUE?
    a. The closer the absolute value of r is to ±1, the closer the predicted values of Y will lie to the regression line.
    b. The further the predicted values lie to the regression line, the less the error of prediction of the dependent variable based upon the independent variable.
    c. The closer the absolute value of r is to zero, the closer the predicted values of Y will lie to the regression line.
    d. The closer the predicted values lie to the regression line, the less the error of prediction of the dependent variable based upon the independent variable
    e. Both “a” and “d” are correct

58. Your colleague is reading an article that reports "R" (an upper case "R") rather than the commonly used lower case "r". He asks you what this means.
    a. This is a multiple correlation coefficient utilized when more than 2 variables help determine the variables' relationship(s).
    b. This is a Spearman rho or Spearman rank order "r" which is utilized for determining correlations for non-parametric variables.
    c. This is a Pearson product moment "r" or Pearson correlation coefficient which is utilized for determining correlations for parametric variables.
    d. This is the coefficient of determination which represents the percentage of variation in one variable that is accounted for by another variable.

59. A randomized, controlled trial evaluated the risk for stroke in patients with various blood pressures. Post treatment systolic blood pressures for this trial ranged from 135mmHg to 190mmHg. Based upon a simple linear regression analysis, it appears that, in this range of blood pressures (135-190mmHg), stroke risk decreased by 4% for every 2mmHg decrease in blood pressure. The investigators conclude that not only can decreasing systolic blood pressures to the lower end of the range in this trial decrease stroke risk by 40% in the US population, but they also state that they estimate another 10-20% reduction in stroke risk could be realized if systolic blood pressures are lowered to 115mmHg. Which of the following is your best response to the authors' conclusions?
    a. Since we do not know what will happen to a relationship beyond the obtained data, the line of best fit should *not* be extrapolated beyond 135mmHg.
    b. This seems like a logical deduction so it is completely appropriate to extrapolate the data beyond the extreme data points of the trial.
    c. Since we have current hypertension guidelines, we should *not* recommend lowering blood pressure below the current recommendation of 140/90mmHg for patients with diabetes.
    d. Since we have current hypertension guidelines, we should *not* recommend lowering blood pressure below the current recommendation of 130/80mmHg for patients with systolic dysfunction heart failure.

60. A study was performed evaluating a possible correlation between the use of the herbal product Goldenseal and changes in pain relief (via a 10 point pain scale). Which type of correlation analysis should be utilized in this study?
    a. Pearson
    b. Spearman's
    c. Linear
    d. Cox

61. A study was performed evaluating a possible correlation between the use of the herbal product Goldenseal and changes in blood pressure. Which type of correlation analysis should be utilized in this study?
    a. Pearson
    b. Spearman's
    c. Linear
    d. Cox

(for the next 2 questions)

A retrospective study produces correlation/regression analysis between sedentary lifestyle and risk for cardiovascular (CV) disease, reporting an r = 0.75.

62. Which of the following statement(s) is (are) TRUE?
    a. An r = 0.75 implies causation more than an r = 0.56
    b. An r = 0.56 implies causation less than an r = 0.75
    c. An r = 0.9 implies causation more than an r = 0.1
    d. A higher r-value does not imply causation any more than a lower r-value

63. Which of the following is correct?
    a. 75% of CV disease is caused by a sedentary lifestyle
    b. 56% of CV disease is not explained by a sedentary lifestyle
    c. 75% of CV disease is not caused by a sedentary lifestyle
    d. 25% of CV disease is not explained by a sedentary lifestyle
    e. 56% of CV disease may be explained by a sedentary lifestyle

64. The EDIC study was a 10 year prospective observational study that started at the end of the 7 year DCCT trial. The DCCT trial evaluated tight vs non-tight glucose control in Type 1 DM patients. In the 10 year EDIC observational study period, all patients received tight glucose control. The group that received tight glucose control during the 7 year DCCT trial showed a significant decrease in risk for cardiovascular outcomes 10 years after the DCCT trial ended relative to the patients who did not receive tight control during the 7 year DCCT trial. Based upon the Cox Proportional Hazards Analysis table, which was the most influential variable in decreasing the risk for cardiovascular outcomes in the EDIC study?

Proportional-Hazards Model of Covariates on Risk of Cardiovascular Outcomes	
Time-Dependent Covariate	Adjusted for Time-Dependent Covariate:
	Hazard Ratio (95% CI)
None	0.53 (0.34-0.83)
Renal disease (yes vs no)	0.54 (0.34-0.84)
Microalbuminuria (yes vs no)	0.62 (0.39-0.97)
Albuminuria (yes vs no)	0.58 (0.37-0.91)
Mean glycosylated hemoglobin value (A1c)	
Per 10% increase	0.84 (0.43-1.64)

    a. Renal function
    b. Management of proteinuria
    c. Microalbuminuria
    d. Albuminuria
    e. Diabetes management

Answers to Study Questions:

55. b - $r = 0.65$, so the coefficient of determination (r^2) = 0.58. This means that 58% of HTN may be explained by a high sodium diet. The coefficient of non-determination ($1-r^2$) = 0.42, which means that 42% of HTN may not be explained by a high sodium diet. The existence of a statistical association with correlation or regression analysis is not in itself evidence of causality. To explain causality, considerations such as the type of analysis being performed must be addressed. (i.e., case-control vs cohort vs RCT)

56. a

57. e

58. a

59. a

60. b - A 10 point pain scale is an ordinal data scale (scored on a continuum, without a consistent level of magnitude of difference between ranks), so Spearman's would be appropriate for this analysis. Pearson would be appropriate for correlations of parametric data. There are no correlation analyses with the names of "Linear" or "Cox". These are types of regression analysis. Linear regression analysis is used for parametric data and Cox regression analysis is used for nominal data.

61. a - Changes in blood pressure per mmHg increments is parametric data (scored on a continuum with a consistent level of magnitude of difference between data points), so Pearson would be appropriate for this analysis. Spearman would be appropriate for correlations of ordinal data. There are no correlation analyses with the names of "Linear" or "Cox". These are types of regression analysis. Linear regression analysis is used for parametric data and Cox regression analysis is used for nominal data.

62. d - The existence of a statistical association with correlation or regression analysis is not in itself evidence of causality. To explain causality, considerations such as the type of analysis being performed must be addressed. (i.e., case-control vs cohort vs RCT)

63. e - $r = 0.75$, so the coefficient of determination (r^2) = 0.56. This means that 56% of CV disease risk may be explained by a sedentary lifestyle. The coefficient of non-determination ($1-r^2$) = 0.44, which means that 44% of CV disease risk may not be explained by a sedentary lifestyle. The existence of a statistical association with correlation or regression analysis is not in itself evidence of causality. To explain causality, considerations such as the type of analysis being performed must be addressed. (i.e., case-control vs cohort vs RCT)

64. e - When the investigators evaluated the data for patients with versus without Renal Disease, Microalbuminuria, or Albuminuria, the hazards ratio (HR) changed, but not much as for the change of 10% increase in A1c (point estimate increased from 0.53 to 0.84). Note also that when the investigators controlled for Renal Disease, Microalbuminuria, or Albuminuria (i.e., negating the influence of each of these independent variables), the difference in CV outcomes was still statistically significant because the CI still did not include 1.0. However, when the investigators controlled for the 10% increase in A1c (i.e., negating the influence of difference in A1c), the difference in CV outcomes was no longer statistically significant because the CI included 1.0 (HR 0.84 (0.43-1.64). Therefore, most of the reason for a difference in CV endpoints was secondary to differences in A1c. The patients whose glucoses were always tightly controlled (the full 17 years) were less likely to have CV endpoints relative to the patients whose glucoses were not tightly controlled during the first 7 yrs of the DCCT trial (i.e., only had tight control for the last 10 years of the analysis).

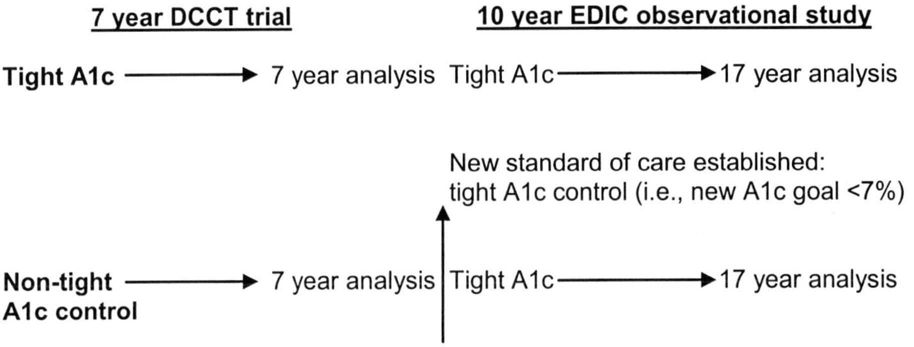

<u>7 year DCCT trial</u> | <u>10 year EDIC observational study</u>

Tight A1c → 7 year analysis | Tight A1c → 17 year analysis

New standard of care established:
tight A1c control (i.e., new A1c goal <7%)

Non-tight A1c control → 7 year analysis | Tight A1c → 17 year analysis

At the end of the 7 year DCCT trial, tight control was found to decrease risk for microvascular outcomes, so it became the new standard of care; all Type 1 DM patients were changed to tight control: new A1c goal <7%.

Note that the only interventional difference between the groups was the difference in tightly vs non-tightly controlling A1c during the first 7 years of the total 17 years of data that were analyzed. (i.e., only during the 7 year DCCT trial)

Ok, I know it's pretty sad or maybe even scary that it takes almost an entire page to explain the answer to one question. However, clinicians will see these types of post-trial observational studies and regression analyses when evaluating medical literature and it's very important to understand how to interpret and apply these properly.

PART 7: Error, Bias, Confounding, Randomization, Controls, Validity

Accuracy vs Precision:

"Accuracy refers to the closeness of the observation to the actual or true value. Precision (or reproducibility) refers to the closeness of repeated measurements."[42]

Error vs Bias:

Error occurs when mistakes that neither systematically under- nor over-estimate effect size are made.[13] This is sometimes referred to as random error. An example would be if a coin were tossed 10 times, yielding 8 "heads", leading one to conclude that the probability of heads is 80%.[13]

Bias refers to systematic errors or flaws in study design which lead to incorrect results.[11,12,13] In other words, bias is "error with direction" leading to systematic under- or over-estimation of effect size.[13]

- "**Bias in the Publication Process**"[13]
  - **Funding** sources: pharmaceutical company research may be viewed by some as promotional.[13] Pharmaceutical sponsorship in and of itself is not necessarily a weakness or a source of bias unless the company controls data collection, analysis, and/or rights to deny the data's publication. Also note if the authors have received gifts, funding, sponsorship or company agreement which may introduce bias.
  - **Publication bias**: studies that show statistically or clinically significant results are more likely to be published. A problem for meta-analysis authors is "negative study bias" where studies failing to detect differences between groups are less often published and are therefore more difficult to find for inclusion into the meta-analysis.[13]
  - "**Investigator or sponsor bias**"[13]: studies conducted by well-known researchers are more likely to be published in some cases.[13]
  - "**Reviewer bias**"[13]
  - "**Small study bias**"[13]: Small studies are less likely to be published in some cases, especially if the results are unimpressive.[13]

- **Adherence (aka compliance) bias** "occurs when patients are more compliant with one treatment relative to another treatment."[29] One example would be comparing a drug that is dosed daily to one that is dosed twice daily. Another example would be comparing a drug with a good adverse effect profile to one that causes intolerable adverse effects.

- **Prevalence bias**: prevalence can change when there are significant "time lapses between exposure or diagnosis and enrollment" in a study.[29]

- **Selection bias** is most common in case-control studies, but can occur in cohort studies. With this type of bias, through flawed methodology, investigators select who will and who will not participate in a study.[9,12]

  - "**Inclusion in study** depends upon exposure of interest."[11]

    - Examples:

      - "Women taking oral contraceptives (OC) might be more likely to examine their breasts."[11,12,13] This will lead to earlier and more frequent detection of Breast CA.

      - Looking at only class 1 or 2 HF rather than all four classes.

  - "**Participation bias** in a study"[11,12]

    - Examples:

      - Disease linked to socioeconomic status, like asthma: using a phone or computer for interviews would select out those who do not have a phone or computer.[9] These may be the very people one wants to capture for a study. This flawed methodology could decrease study power or weaken the ability to apply results to other patient populations and/or systems (i.e., decrease external validity/generalizability: see page 126).

      - "Pap smears and Cervical Cancer: controls selected through random phone calls during business hours may exclude employed controls. Unemployed subjects may be less likely to get a pap smear because they lack insurance.[11,12,13]

  - **Admission rate bias** "occurs when hospital admission rates differ between the groups studied."[29]

  - **Non-response bias** "occurs when subjects fail to respond to a survey or questionnaire."[29]

  - **Membership bias** "occurs when patients have more than 1 characteristic in common" and this characteristic "is related to the disease under investigation."[29]

- "**Diagnostic or Detection bias**"[11] Cases more readily detected.
    - For example, estrogen replacement therapy (ERT) may increase the likelihood for vaginal bleeding, leading to a doctor's examination and earlier uterine CA detection and diagnosis."[11,12,13]
- **Insensitive measure bias** "occurs when the instruments used are not sensitive enough to detect the disease of interest."[29] For example, glucometers from 10 years ago are not as accurate in detecting hyper- and hypoglycemia as are currently available meters. This would decrease ability to compare glucose endpoints between older and newer studies.
- **Procedure bias** "occurs when all treatment groups do not receive the same diagnostic procedures. This leads to increased detection of the disease in one group."[29]
    - For example, a new technique for diagnosis is developed that detects colon cancer sooner, resulting in improved care and increased survival relative to prior years when older diagnostics were used.[29]

Bias that "can falsely identify or inflate risk factors" include recall and interviewer bias.[11] These are quite undesirable and should definitely be avoided.

- **Recall bias**: the classic example is an epidemiological study of birth defects secondary to medications.[9,11,12,13] Moms who delivered babies without complications would less likely remember what meds they took relative to moms who did experience complications.[9,11,12,13,15]
- **Observer bias** may occur "when subjects are observed by multiple untrained investigators."[29] It is most problematic with "open" or unblinded study designs.
- **Interviewer bias**: "interviews are not conducted in a uniform manner for all study participants."[9] For example, some subjects are questioned more intensely regarding exposure, leading questions are asked, or some charts are reviewed more thoroughly for exposure.[11,12,13] This can be minimized by scripted questions and dialog or provision of interviewer training.[12,15]
- **Misclassification bias**: patient is thought to have been exposed to a certain agent or have a disease, but has not been exposed or does not have the disease.[9,15] In the example of a case-control study, classifying one as having a disease (case) when he/she doesn't.[15] In the example of a cohort study, classifying a patient as having been exposed when he/she has not been exposed. Misclassification bias may bias in favor of one group over another or in favor of finding no difference between the groups

- **Random Misclassification bias**: "errors in exposure or disease history in both cases and controls." With random misclassification, errors occur equally in each group, thereby decreasing the true effect of exposure and biasing towards finding no difference between evaluated groups.[11,12]

- **Channeling bias (aka confounding by indication)** occurs when subjects are "channeled" into a particular intervention or group. For example, "people who are at the greatest risk of developing an adverse drug reaction (ADR) may be systematically given a drug that claims to cause less of that ADR. Any true difference between agents in terms of that ADR is diluted because only the people who were at the greatest risk for developing the ADR received the drug."[12,15]

  - Patients who had a gastrointestinal (GI) bleed while taking a traditional non-steroidal anti-inflammatory drug (NSAID) may be "channeled" into trying a "safer" NSAID that is proposed to cause fewer GI adverse effects. Since a prior GI bleed increases the risk for a subsequent GI bleed, any benefit of the "safer" NSAID may not be demonstrated.

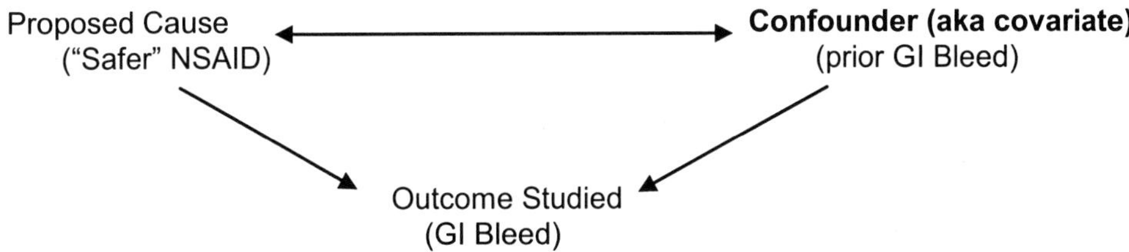

  - Patients who are suicidal, may be "channeled" into receiving a new, less studied, treatment for depression. Since suicidal depression increases the risk for suicide, any benefit of the new depression treatment may not be demonstrated. This may also lead us to believe that the new treatment increases risk for suicide.

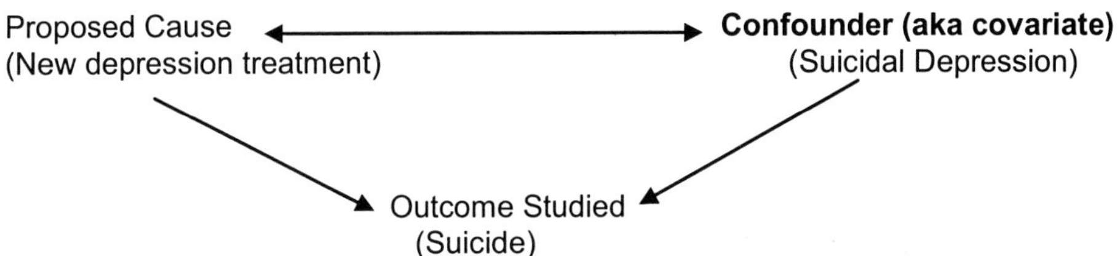

Methods to Minimize Bias

Bias is minimized through a combination of proper study design, methods, and analysis. Proper analysis **cannot** "de-flaw" a study with poor design or methodology.[9]

- **Randomization** is sometimes referred to as allocation. In this process, patients are divided into groups by chance alone such that potential confounders (see pages 120-126) are divided equally among the groups and bias is minimized.[11,12] However, there must be adequate numbers of patients in each group to maximize equal division of confounders. Doing so helps ensure that all within a studied population have an equal and independent opportunity of being selected as part of a sample. This can be carried a step further in that once the person has been selected for a sample, he/she has an equal opportunity of being selected for any of the study arms.

  - **Simple randomization**: an example would be drawing numbers from a hat. Its advantage is that it is simple. Its disadvantage is that if a trial were stopped early, there is no assurance of similar numbers of subjects in each group at any given point in time.

  - **Block randomization** involves randomizing patients into small groups of subjects called blocks. These blocks generally range from 4 to 20 subjects. Block randomization is advantageous in that there are nearly equal numbers of subjects in each group at any point during a trial. Therefore if a trial is stopped early, equal comparisons and more valid conclusions can be made.

  - **Stratified randomization** involves separating subjects into non-overlapping groups called strata, based upon factors that may affect (or confound) study endpoints. This divides potential confounders among groups to minimize their potential influence on study outcome(s). Remember "SR": always Stratify before Randomizing. (see pages 124-126 for more complete explanation)

  - **Combined blocked and stratified randomization** is often used to avoid imbalance of subjects and confounding variables in each study arm. For example, stratifying by study center, combined with blocked randomization, helps minimize imbalance if a study center has to be excluded for the final analysis. (see pages 124-126 for more complete explanation)

- **Proper selection** of study subjects (i.e., proper inclusion and exclusion criteria)[9]

- **Blinding** limits investigators' treating or assessing one group differently from another. It is especially important if there is any degree of subjectivity associated with the outcome(s) being assessed. However, it is expensive and time consuming.[9,11,13] (see pages 120-121 for various types of blinding)

- **Using appropriate controls** allows investigators to minimize outside influences when evaluating a treatment or exposure.[13] (see page 119 for various types of controls)

- **Matching** subjects is a way of minimizing bias and confounding in case-control and sometimes cohort studies. It involves identifying characteristics that are a potential source of bias, and then matching patients based upon those characteristics. Doing so helps minimize the characteristics' influence on the study's findings.[37] However, it takes a lot of time and effort, is difficult to perform in large studies, and may increase type 2 error risk.[9,11] A method that decreases the complexity of matching is **propensity score matching (PSM)**. PSM helps capture relevant, potentially biasing variables and matches based upon those to minimize bias and confounding. It is more efficient and easier to perform than traditional matching and is especially useful in minimizing selection bias.[37,38]

    - Ways matching may increase type 2 error risk.

        - Over-matching occurs when there is a strong association between the matched variable and the variable being evaluated. This will increase type 2 error risk.[11]

        - Do not match based upon factors which are affected by exposure or disease, like signs or symptoms of a disease. Do not match based upon an intermediate step between exposure and outcome. For example, in a study evaluating staph aureus bacteremia and death, avoid matching based upon sepsis because this will increase risk for type 2 error.[11]

- Utilizing **objective study endpoints**.[27]

- Utilizing **proper and accurate means of defining exposure and endpoints**.

- Utilizing **accurate and complete sources of information**.[9]

- **Minimizing loss of subjects** through the end of the study.[13]

- Utilizing **appropriate statistical tests** for data analysis.[9,13]

Controlled vs Non-controlled Studies

Controlled Study: efforts are made to keep the study groups as similar as possible and to minimize outside influences. Ideally, groups will differ only in the factor being studied.[15]

Uncontrolled Study: there is no control group so outside influences may affect study results.[15]

- **Types of Controls**
  - **Placebo control** is not always practical or ethical, but one or more groups receives active treatment(s) while the control group receives a placebo."[13,15]
  - **Historical control** studies are generally less expensive to perform but this design introduces problems with diagnostic, detection, and procedure biases. "Data from a group of subjects receiving the experimental drug or intervention are compared to data from a group of subjects previously treated during a different time period, perhaps in a different place."[15]
  - **Cross-over control** is very efficient at minimizing bias while maximizing power when used appropriately. Each subject serves as his/her own control. Initially, group A receives the experimental drug while group B receives the control (placebo or gold standard treatment). After a washout period, group A receives the control and group B receives the experimental drug.[15]
  - **Standard Treatment (aka Active Treatment) control** is very practical and ethical. Control group subjects receive 'standard' treatment while the other group(s) receive(s) experimental treatment(s). This type of control is used when the investigator wishes to demonstrate that the experimental treatment(s) is/are equally efficacious, non-inferior, or superior to 'standard' treatment.[15]
  - **Within Patient Comparison control** is generally used for dermatological studies. One part of the body is treated with the experimental treatment while another part of the body is treated with either a 'standard' or placebo control.[15]

Blinding

Blinding limits investigators' treating or assessing one group differently from another. It is especially important if there is any degree of subjectivity associated with the outcome(s) being assessed. However, it is expensive and time consuming.

- **Types of Blinding**
  - **Non-blinded** trial: the investigator and subject know what treatment or intervention the subject is receiving. This type of investigation is commonly referred to as an open-label trial.[15]
  - **Single-blind** trial: someone, usually the patient, but in rare cases it may be the investigator, is un-aware of what treatment or intervention the subject is receiving.[15]
  - **Double-blind** trial: neither the investigator nor the subject is aware of what treatment or intervention the subject is receiving.[15]
  - **Double-dummy** trial: if one is comparing two different dosage forms (e.g., intranasal sumatriptan vs injectable sumatriptan), and doesn't want the patient or investigator to know in which arm a patient is participating, then one group would receive intranasal sumatriptan and a placebo injection and the other group would receive intranasal placebo and a sumatriptan injection.[15] Another example would be for a trial evaluating a tablet vs an inhaler.
  - **Triple blind** trial: patients, investigator(s), and statistician are unaware of which treatment or intervention the subject is receiving.[17]
  - **Total blind** trial: patients, investigators, statistician, or anyone who manipulates data, and anyone they contact are unaware of which treatment or intervention the subject is receiving.[17]
- **Some trials that claim to be blinded are not.**
  - A medication may have a distinctive taste, physiologic effect, or adverse effect that un-blinds patients and/or investigators. For example, diuretics increase urination and ACEIs may induce cough, thereby un-blinding both patients and investigators.
  - Trials with an active treatment run-in phase may negate blinding. An active treatment run-in phase is a pre-trial phase during which all potential study subjects receive the active experimental medication(s) prior to acceptance into the trial. During this time, investigators check adherence, tolerance to the experimental medication(s)

- Subjects who received active medication during the run-in phase and placebo during the trial may feel differently or recognize some other difference: cough, dizziness, lightheadedness, headache, edema, or weakness.

- Investigators may note similarities or changes in lab work performed during the active run-in phase versus the actual trial phase. For example, investigators may note hyperkalemia, elevated BUN, or SCr.

Confounding

Confounding occurs when variables, other than the one(s) being studied, influence study results. Confounding variables are difficult to detect sometimes and are linked to study outcome(s) and may be linked to hypothesized cause(s). Validity of a study depends upon how well investigators minimize the influence of confounders.[9,11,15]

Example 1: Atherosclerosis and myocardial infarction (MI, aka heart attack): there is an association between atherosclerosis and smoking, smoking and risk for having a heart attack, and atherosclerosis and risk for having a heart attack. The proposed cause is atherosclerosis and the potential confounder is smoking.

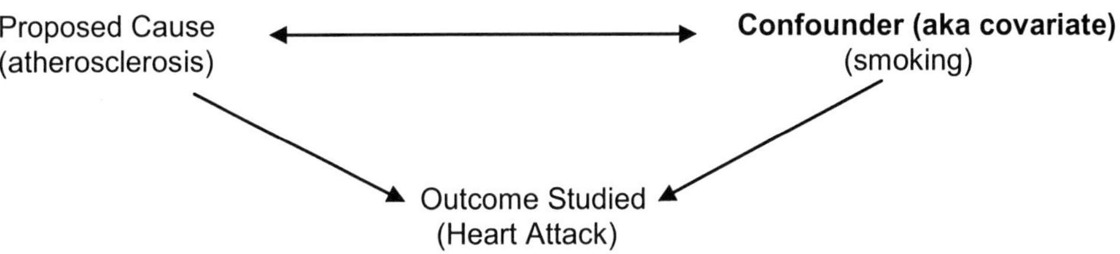

Example 2[12,13]: Steroids and ED visits: one may INCORRECTLY conclude that steroid use in patients with asthma leads to an increase in ED visits if confounders are not considered.

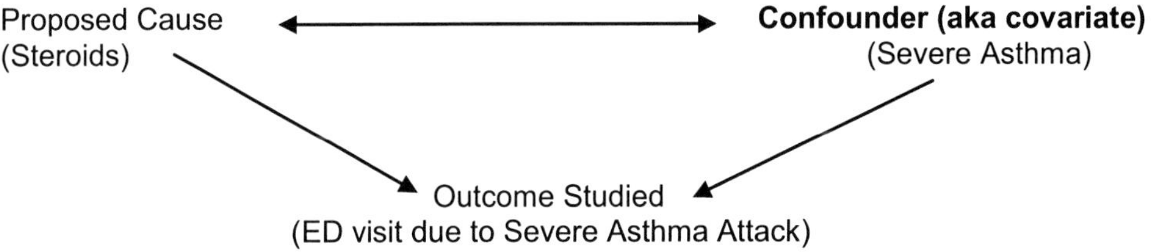

Example 3: Diet and Weight Loss.

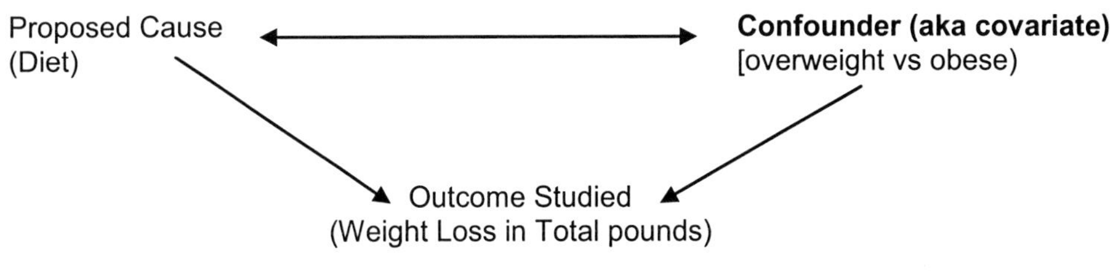

Example 4 is an example of confounding by indication (aka channeling bias). Patients who are suicidal may be "channeled" into receiving a new, less studied, treatment for depression. Since suicidal depression increases the risk for suicide, any benefit of the new depression treatment may not be demonstrated. This may also lead us to believe that the new treatment increases risk for suicide.

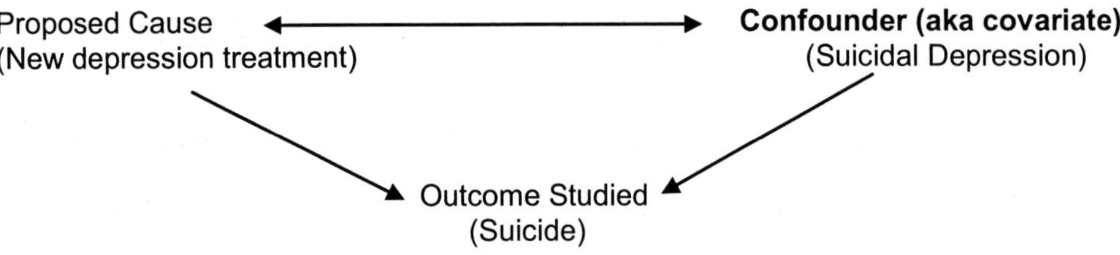

Collinearity is sometimes confused with confounding. Remember that confounders are linked to study outcome(s) and may be linked to hypothesized cause(s). With collinearity, collinear variables are only linked to the hypothesized cause (predictor). Collinear variables have no link to, or effect on, outcome(s).[11]

> For example, patients who smoke are more likely to have matches or a lighter and vice versa. Patients who smoke are more likely to have a heart attack at some point in their lives. However, having matches or a lighter does not increase the risk for having a heart attack. It is simply a marker for smoking.

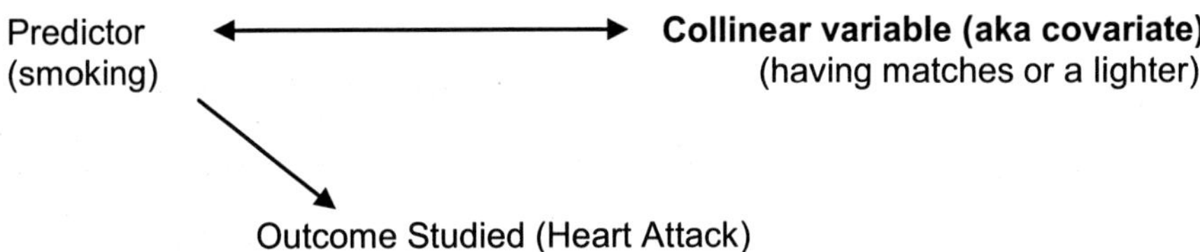

With collinearity, the p-value is "falsely elevated between the predictor and outcome." This can decrease the ability to detect differences between predictor(s) and outcome(s).[11] Study investigators should "identify and remove collinear variables from multivariate models."[11]

Methods to Minimize Confounding

Whereas bias is minimized only through proper study design and methods, **confounding is minimized through the combination of proper study design, methods, and analysis.**[9,11]

- **Design**[9,15]
  - **Randomization**[11,12] as explained in the "Methods to Minimize Bias" section on pages 117-118.
  - **Proper selection** of study subjects (i.e., proper inclusion and exclusion criteria)[9]
  - **Blinding**[9,11,13] as explained in the "Blinding" section on pages 117, 120-121.
  - **Matching** as explained in the "Methods to Minimize Bias" section on page 118.
- **Analysis**[9,15] (ways to account for confounding in analysis)
  - **Stratification** (for baseline risks):[9,11,15, 45]
    - The purpose is to help **divide potential confounders among groups to minimize their potential influence on study outcome(s).**
    - Before randomization, **subjects are separated into non-overlapping groups called strata, based upon factors that may affect (or confound) study endpoints.** Examples of strata that are commonly seen in clinical trials include age, gender, ethnicity, smoking status, study center, concomitant medication use, comorbidities, or disease severity.[45]
    - For example, in a study evaluating the influence of different medications (Med A vs Med B) on stroke risk (cerebrovascular accident – CVA), if there is concern that an imbalance in comorbidities (e.g., diabetes) may influence (or confound) the results, study subjects are first stratified such that the groups have an equal number of diabetes patients in each arm.[11] Within each stratum, subjects are then randomized to different medication arms.[45] Remember "SR": always Stratify before Randomizing.

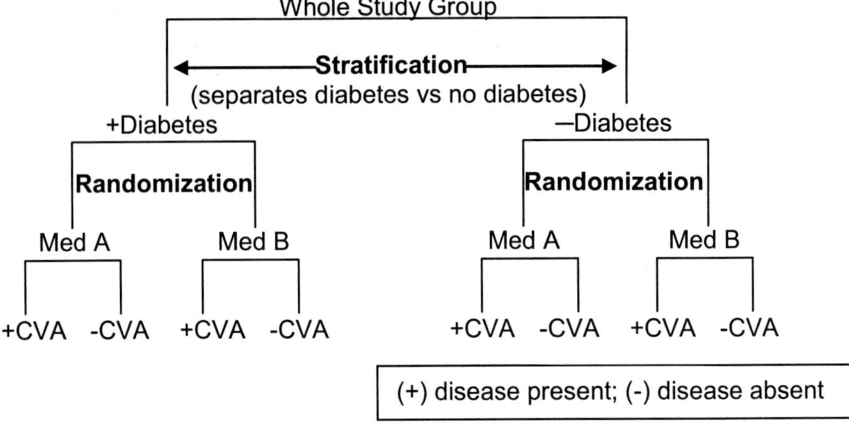

- This helps ensure that possible confounding variables are balanced among study arms.[45]

- Most necessary for…

  - small trials (i.e., trials with a small sample size) since confounding variables less likely to be balanced.[45]

  - large trials that have planned interim analyses since these typically take place when the sample size is still small.[45]

  - trials with subgroup analyses to balance subgroups and force investigators to identify these apriori.[45]

  - trials with a prolonged recruitment period, if prognostic characteristic changes are likely to occur over time.[45]

- Often used with block randomization to avoid imbalance of subjects and confounding variables in each study arm. Stratifying by study center, combined with blocked randomization, helps minimize imbalance if a study center has to be excluded for the final analysis.[45]

- "Stratification has limits."[11]
  - As one stratifies, subgroup sample sizes decrease, so one's ability to detect meaningful influences in each subgroup will also decrease.[11]

  - It is "difficult to present results of multiple stratification" since "sample sizes in subgroups become smaller the more one stratifies".[11]

- It adds a step before randomization which increases time to a patient's receiving treatment. This may be unethical in an emergency. (e.g., in an ER setting when emergent treatment is needed)

- **Multivariate (or multiple) Regression Analysis (MRA – aka post-stratification)** is a possible solution.[9,15,45]

  - Outcomes are adjusted for possible confounders (e.g., differences in baseline patient characteristics).[45]

  - As discussed in the regression section, "multiple predictor variables (aka independent variables) can be used to predict outcomes (aka dependent variables)."[11]

    - For example, the national cholesterol guidelines utilize multiple (multivariate) regression to help establish atherosclerotic cardiovascular disease (ASCVD) risk for patients based upon population data. A patient's ASCVD risk is the dependent variable because its estimate "depends upon" multiple independent variables. The independent variables include gender, race, age, total cholesterol, HDL-cholesterol, smoking status, systolic blood pressure, whether or not a patient is being treated for hypertension, or has diabetes. These multiple independent variables are used to help predict a patient's ASCVD risk.

- As previously discussed, **various types of ANOVAs** help account for confounding. (multivariate ANOVAs for non-paired data, and Two-Way Repeated Measures ANOVA for paired data)

Validity

- Internal validity addresses how well a study was conducted: if appropriate methods were used to minimize bias and confounding and ensure that exposures, interventions, and outcomes were measured correctly.[9] This includes ensuring the study accurately tested and measured what it claims to have tested and measured.[9,13,15] Internal validity directly affects external validity; **without internal validity, a study has no external validity.**[15]

- External validity: presuming internal validity, external validity addresses the application of study findings to other groups, patients, systems, or the general population.[9,13,15]

- "A high degree of internal validity is often achieved at the expense of external validity."[13] For example, excluding diabetic hypertensive patients from a study may provide very clean statistical endpoints. However, clinicians who treat mainly diabetic hypertensive patients may be unable to utilize the results from such a trial.[13]

Study Questions:

(For the next 3 questions)
A colleague wants your opinion on how to minimize bias and/or confounding while conducting a trial of a new cholesterol medication.

65. Which of the following would <u>not</u> help?
    a. Randomization and blinding
    b. Utilizing a control group
    c. Restricting certain patients from the trial
    d. Minimizing loss of patients to follow-up
    e. Maximizing external validity while minimizing internal validity.

66. The colleague also wants your opinion on how to control for bias and/or confounding in the analysis section of the trial. Which of the following would <u>not</u> help?
    a. Stratification
    b. Multivariate regression analysis
    c. Utilizing ANOVA for non-parametric endpoints
    d. Utilizing chi-square for nominal endpoints

67. If your colleague utilizes appropriate methodology and a broad population base for inclusion in the trial there will be ___________.
    a. Strong internal validity
    b. Strong external validity
    c. Strong internal and external validity

68. An unblinded (open-label) trial was performed to assess the effect of a new oral anticoagulant compared to heparin for the treatment of acute deep venous thromboembolism (DVT). The trial included 500 patients in each treatment group. The patients received the new anticoagulant daily or adjusted dose heparin for the first 5 days of therapy. The trial concluded that patients in the new anticoagulant group had no higher chance of a subsequent DVT than did the patients in the heparin group. Based upon this trial your team should:
    a. Treat any patients meeting the inclusion criteria of the study with the new anticoagulant.
    b. Request a case control study to assure validity of this trial.
    c. Examine the study for bias.
    d. Evaluate the authors to help determine if the new anticoagulant may be beneficial in the patients treated in your facility.

69. *(complete the following)* The national cholesterol guidelines utilized study outcomes data to estimate atherosclerotic cardiovascular disease (ASCVD) risk based upon gender, race, age, total cholesterol, HDL-cholesterol, smoking status, systolic blood pressure, whether or not a patient is being treated for hypertension, or has diabetes. This is a type of _________ analysis.
    a. ANOVA
    b. Pearson correlation
    c. Spearman correlation
    d. Simple linear regression
    e. Multivariate regression

(for the next 2 questions)
An investigator conducts a case-control study evaluating various exposures for patients who were diagnosed with a rare form of cancer. 30 cases have been noted over the last 10 years. Surviving patients and their families will be interviewed.

70. Which of the following is most likely to present a problem with this study?
    a. Selection bias
    b. Random error
    c. Recall bias
    d. Carryover effect
    e. Publication bias

71. How might an investigator minimize bias with this study design?
    a. Match cases with appropriately selected controls
    b. Randomize patients
    c. Only evaluate 10 of the 30 cases
    d. Utilize a double blind trial design
    e. None of the above would be effective ways to minimize this trial's problem.

72. A large randomized controlled trial is funded by a major pharmaceutical company. What are reasons why this may not be a problem "in and of itself"?
    a. The investigators point out that the company does not have the legal rights to refuse publication regardless of the results.
    b. There are no company associates or company associated investigators affiliated with the independent analysis and review team which was used for all analyses, interim or otherwise.
    c. None of the company associates are voting members of the research team.
    d. All of the above [a, b, and c] are reasons the funding source is not necessarily a source of bias in this trial.
    e. Regardless of the safeguards in place, utilizing a funding source other than the NIH (National Institutes of Health) or some other altruistic funding source is a major source of bias.

73. Which of the following statements is FALSE?
    a. Small study bias is a type of publication bias.
    b. Investigator or sponsor bias is a type of publication bias.
    c. If interviews are conducted via phone and/or e-mail, a bias against inclusion of lower socioeconomic patients may be a problem.
    d. Channeling bias is a type of confounding.
    e. All of the above are correct statements.

Answers to Study Questions:

65. e - Without internal validity, there is no external validity.

66. c - ANOVA would be appropriate for parametric endpoint analysis, not non-parametric endpoint analysis.

67. c - Utilizing appropriate methodology helps increase internal validity. Including a broad population helps increase external validity. However, remember that without internal validity, there is not external validity; weak internal validity (improper methodology), negates external validity (applying findings to patients and populations).

68. c - This is a non-blinded trial (open-label), so it is subject to more bias than would a blinded trial, especially if the investigator(s) and/or funding source(s) had any conflicts of interest: monetary gain, notoriety, etc. Therefore, one needs to evaluate this study very carefully to try and identify potential biases that may have influenced the results before utilizing this trial data for treating any patients, even if they met the inclusion criteria of the trial. If the trial had internal validity, evaluating the subjects of the trial (not the authors as was the choice provided in answer "d"), would help determine if the new anticoagulant may be useful for the patients' in one's facility (external validity). Case-control studies are very weak with regard to establishing causality, so would not help assure validity of this trial.

69. e - The national cholesterol guidelines utilize multiple (or multivariate) regression to help establish atherosclerotic cardiovascular disease (ASCVD) risk for patients based upon population data. A patient's ASCVD risk is the dependent variable because its estimate "depends upon" multiple independent variables. The independent variables include gender, race, age, total cholesterol, HDL-cholesterol, smoking status, systolic blood pressure, whether or not a patient is being treated for hypertension, or has diabetes. These multiple independent variables are used to help predict a patient's ASCVD risk.

70. c - Surviving patients and their families are more likely to "recall" past exposures that may have increased the risk for cancer. Controls are less likely to "recall" exposures since they did not have cancer and were therefore not as concerned about or focused on remembering to what they were or were not exposed.

71. a - Matching subjects is a way of minimizing bias and confounding in case-control studies. It involves identifying characteristics that are a potential source of bias, and then matching patients based upon those characteristics. Doing so helps minimize the characteristics' influence on the study's findings.

72. d

73. e

Part 8: Study Design

Prospective vs Retrospective

- **Prospective Study**: subjects are followed forward in time from a specified time point, data are collected and then outcomes (endpoints) are measured and analyzed. Examples include randomized controlled trials (RCTs) and truly prospective cohorts (where the exposure takes place in the present or future).

- **Retrospective Study**: investigator(s) look(s) back in time to collect and analyze data. Examples include case report, case series, case-control, retrospective cohort, and the type of prospective cohort where the exposure occurred in the past.

Causality

Finding a statistically significant relationship in a study does <u>not</u> prove causality.[11]

Several things must be considered when assessing causality.

- **Study design, methodology, and analysis are the <u>most</u> important considerations.**

- **Prior probability (consistency of results with previous work by other investigators) and strength of the statistical and/or clinically meaningful association(s) are also very important considerations.**

- Biologic plausibility or theory supporting the conduction of the study.[9,11]

- Temporal relationship: the outcome takes place after the exposure or intervention.[9,11]

- Dose response relationships.[9,11]

Study Design and Relative Causality

One of the most important considerations for assessing causality is study design.

The following is a list noting relative strength of causal relationships and confidence in study results based upon study designs (starting from the strongest design) [9,13]

- **Randomized controlled trial (RCT)**: This is interventional, experimental, and universally accepted as the strongest design for establishing causality when conducted correctly.[9,11,13]

- **Meta-Analysis (MA) or systematic review**: the relative strength of causality for MA or systematic review is controversial.[9] Some are of the opinion that if a these are performed with solely well conducted RCTs, their ability to determine causality is stronger than that of a cohort study, but weaker than that of a RCT. Others think that including solely well conducted RCTs would make these as strong as or stronger than a RCT.

- **Cohort study**: epidemiological, observational designs. Analytical, but not interventional. Sometimes referred to as outcomes or follow-up studies.[9,11,13]

  - **Truly Prospective Cohort**: exposure in the present/future, endpoint in future.

  - **Prospective Cohort**: exposure occurred in the past, endpoint in the future

  - **Retrospective Cohort**: exposure and endpoint occurred in the past.

- **Case-control study**: epidemiological, observational design. Analytical, but not interventional.[9,11,13]

- **Cross-sectional study (aka prevalence study)**[44] "survey characteristics of a population at a given time and are particularly useful for measuring the prevalence of a disease or event. Transient effects or biases are possible because these only measure prevalence at a single point in time"[29]

- **Case series**: This is simply multiple case reports and is neither analytical nor interventional.[9,13]

- **Case report**: This is the weakest design and is neither analytical nor interventional.[9,13]

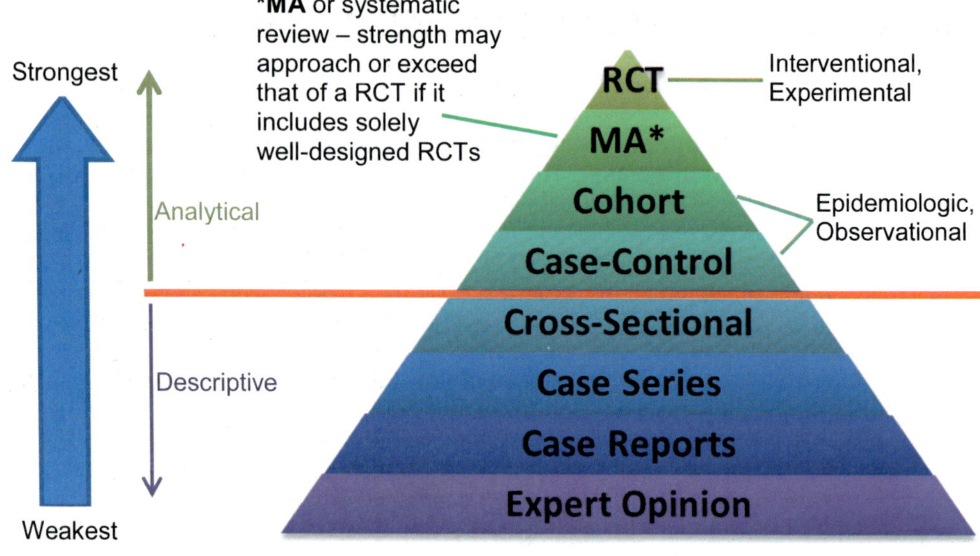
*MA or systematic review – strength may approach or exceed that of a RCT if it includes solely well-designed RCTs
Strongest
Weakest
Analytical
Descriptive
RCT
MA*
Cohort
Case-Control
Cross-Sectional
Case Series
Case Reports
Expert Opinion
Interventional, Experimental
Epidemiologic, Observational

Case-Control Study (aka "Risk Factor Studies")[9]:

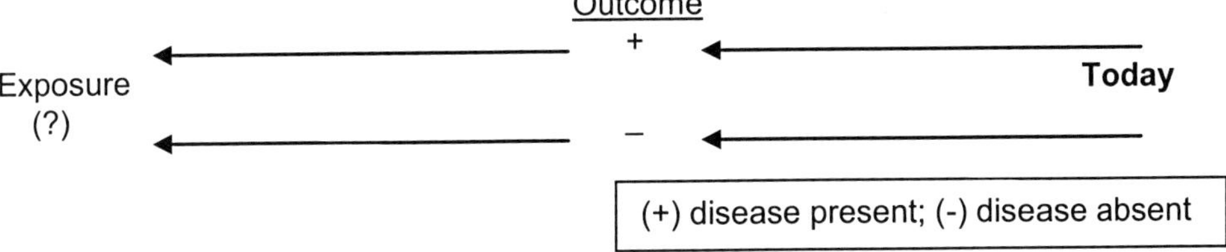

This is a retrospective design study that **identifies** patients **based upon OUTCOME or DISEASE and is therefore good for rare outcomes or diseases.**[9,12] Similar control group patients are desirable, but unequal sample sizes are very common.[9,11,13] Up to 3-4 controls per case help minimize bias and confounding and increase power.[9] This is because there are confounding variables (diseases, medications, exposures, etc.) with controls about which the investigators don't know. Having more controls (3-4) minimizes the influence of these confounders. More than 4 controls per case will not usually increase power any more than 3-4 controls per case.[9] Controls should be selected independently of exposure status and from the same time period as the cases.[11,13] Efforts should be made to avoid selecting controls that are more or less likely to have an exposure than the source population.[11,13]

- Benefits
    - Efficiently identifies multiple, possible causes (exposures) for uncommon or slow-developing outcomes or diseases.[9,11,13]
    - Can use in diseases with long latencies. (e.g., Alzheimer's)[11,13]
    - Requires a smaller sample size than cohorts or RCTs. [e.g., diethylstilbestrol (DES) and clear cell vaginal adenocarcinoma, 8 cases, 42 controls][9]
    - Inexpensive and quick.[9,11,13]
- Problems
    - Inappropriate for rare exposures. Use cohort design instead.[9,11]
    - Inaccurate in determining temporal relationships between exposure and disease since both took place in the past.[11,13] This inaccuracy prevents computation of incidence, so only an estimate of incidence (odds ratio) can be calculated.[11,13]
    - Even with proper planning and execution, bias and confounding prevent establishment of causation since disease and exposure occurred in the past. Case-control is therefore only hypothesis generating and **<u>not</u>** hypothesis

proving.[9,11,13] An exception may be in cases of safety (like adverse effects) where risk clearly outweighs benefit.

  - However, utilizing a nested case control design can help decrease the risk for confounding by indication since its data are generally collected from a well-defined, large cohort and it usually restricts inclusion to patients with similar characteristics.[37]

- Selecting controls (matching) can be a major challenge (almost impossible sometimes).[9,11] Investigators want their controls to represent the source population, but the controls may have influencing factors of which the investigators are unaware. Also, if cases are over-matched, type 2 error risk will increase.[11]

Cohort Studies

Retrospective Cohort (aka Outcomes or Epidemiologic Study)[9]:

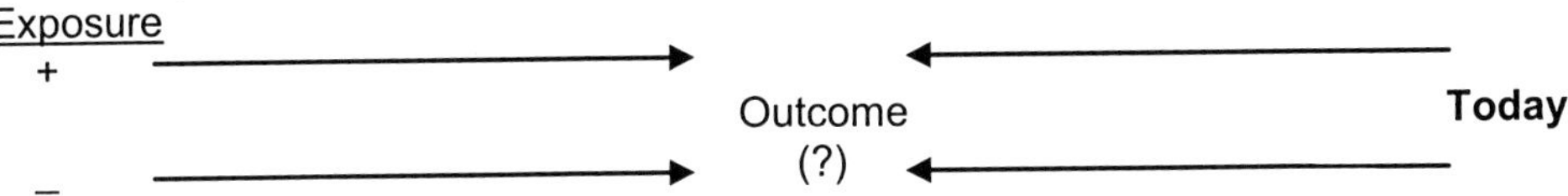

Prospective Cohort (aka Outcomes or Epidemiologic Study)[9]:

Prospective cohort that is retrospective in nature because the exposure(s) took place in the past.[9] This is the most common type of prospective cohort.

Truly prospective cohort is very rare and depicted below[13]:

Exposure

+

Today

Outcome(?)

–

- Benefits
  - Subjects are identified based upon exposure. This allows investigators to identify multiple outcomes or diseases that may be caused by uncommon exposures.[9,12]
  - Good for studying "frequent" outcomes or diseases like atherosclerosis.[11,13]
  - Subject to less bias and confounding than case-control.[9,11,12,13] (particularly in prospective cohort)
  - Generally able to accurately calculate incidence of disease.[11,13]

- Can define temporal trends between exposure and disease (i.e., time to disease).[11,13] May use survival analysis (Kaplan Meier or Cox Proportion) to account for time.

- Note the relative strength with regard to minimizing bias and confounding, accuracy in calculating incidence, and defining temporal trends:

    - Truly prospective cohort > prospective cohort > retrospective cohort

- Less expensive than RCT.

- Can utilize propensity scored matching (PSM) to minimize selection bias. However, PSM is still not randomization. It can only account for identified covariates.

- Problems

  - Inappropriate for rare outcomes or diseases. Use case-control instead.

  - Requires larger sample size than case-control design.[9]

  - More expensive and time consuming than case-control study.[9,11,13] In the case of a prospective cohort, investigators are waiting for a disease or outcome to occur.[9]

  - Loss of patients to follow-up is an issue for prospective cohorts. All one can do is try to minimize this.[11]

  - Exposure is not controlled by the investigator.

  - Subject to bias and confounding. (e.g., some charts may be scrutinized more closely than others, different diagnostic criteria, etc.)[11] Defining cohort characteristics is very important in minimizing bias and confounding (time periods, geographic areas, definition of exposure, diagnostic criteria, etc.).[11]

  - **Hawthorne effect** with prospective cohort. If patients know they are being followed, their behavior patterns improve. (improved adherence with their medication regimen, diet, exercise, etc.) This may either falsely increase or decrease detected differences among study groups.

  - Although propensity scored matching (PSM) can help minimize selection bias, it is still not randomization. It can only account for identified covariates.

Randomized Controlled Trial (RCT)

Parallel design of the RCT is "preferred for acute diseases or for diseases in which treatment is curative."[29]

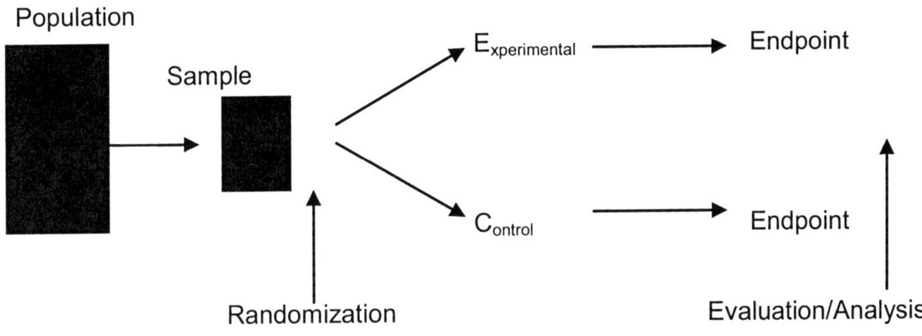

Cross-over design of the RCT is useful when there is wide, inter-patient variability.

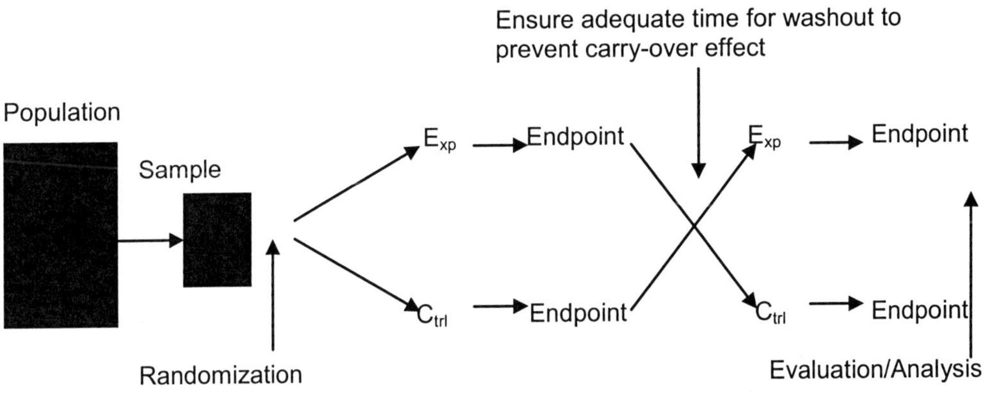

- Cross-over design considerations
  - Cross-overs work well for pharmacokinetic trials or trials for chronic, stable conditions or diseases like osteoarthritis, hypertension, or diabetes.[29] Since each patient serves as his or her own control, sample size requirement, cost, and treatment group variability are minimized.[29]

- Cross-overs are ***not*** appropriate for unstable diseases like asthma or allergic rhinitis since patients may improve or relapse at any time regardless of intervention. For example, if a trial evaluates two interventions, drug A vs drug B, in treating asthma, symptoms can be more severe during treatment with drug A than with drug B simply because of seasonal symptom variation rather than the intervention.[29]

- Cross-overs are ***not*** suitable for "acute conditions, such as postoperative pain or infections."[29]

- Cross-overs are ***not*** appropriate for certain types of treatment questions: for example, treatment of nausea and/or vomiting in chemotherapy trials. This is because response to the first antiemetic evaluated will influence the response to the second antiemetic. Also, there may be cases where cross-overs are unethical or impractical: for example, smoking cessation trials. This is because it would be unethical to ask patients to re-initiate smoking during the second phase of the trial if they quit smoking during the first phase.

- Watch for carry-over effect due to inadequate washout time. "A typical washout period should last at least 5 half-lives of the study drug or its active metabolite to allow for its complete elimination from the body."[29]

- Considerations for both parallel and cross-over RCTs:
  - Is the sample representative of patients in whom clinicians would like to apply the trial results?[9]
  - Were secondary outcomes identified beforehand?
  - **Surrogate markers**: do these tell us anything useful about clinical outcomes or outcomes that matter to patients?[9] The difference between a covariate and surrogate marker is...
    - A **surrogate marker** is an endpoint measurement that is something other than what an investigator truly desires to measure. For example, for many years BP trials concentrated on measuring BP lowering. However, this is no longer adequate. What hypertension investigators really want to know now is how much does a BP medication lower morbidity & mortality (clinical endpoint) relative to standard of care BP meds. So in this case BP lowering differences would be a surrogate marker for a new BP med.

- A **covariate** can be either a...

  - Confounder (aka confounding covariate): a variable, other than the outcome being studied, which influences study results. It is linked to study outcome(s) and may be linked to hypothesized cause(s).

    or a...

  - Collinear variable which is only linked to the hypothesized cause (predictor), without any link to, or effect on, outcome(s).[11]

- **Composite Endpoints (CEs):** "CEs combine the data of more than 1 outcome into a single analysis. A CE of hospitalization, worsening symptoms, or death might be used as the primary endpoint in a trial of drugs for heart failure. Any significant differences between groups for this outcome would imply that patients who receive the study therapy are less likely to experience worsening symptoms, hospital admission, or death. A criticism of this approach is that only 1 or 2 of the outcomes measured in the CE is/are truly different between groups. Differences observed in the remaining 2 or 3 outcomes factored into the CE may not be significant. In particular, the combination of subjective (e.g., worsening symptoms) and objective (e.g., death) outcomes into a single endpoint contributes to unreliable conclusions. A more optimal approach would be to design the trial to assess individual outcomes, but this may not be feasible, affordable, or of interest."[27]

- **Sub-group analyses are hypothesis forming, not hypothesis proving**.[11]

- Benefits for both parallel and cross-over RCTs:

  - **RCT is the best design for establishing causality** since it divides potential confounders evenly among study groups and minimizes outside influences when evaluating interventions.[9,11]

  - Blinding helps minimize bias, helping ensure equal treatment among study groups, and producing more precise and trustworthy results.

- Problems for both parallel and cross-over RCTs:

  - Time/Labor intensive and very expensive.[11]

    - Ensuring methodology is ethical and feasible such that it can be approved by designated Institutional Review Boards (IRB).[11] Balancing desired data collection and ethics can sometimes be difficult.

- Utilization of an independent data and safety monitoring committee is needed to assess early discontinuation of a study and help ensure patient safety.

- Ability to generalize results to a particular patient population (external validity) may be limited depending upon inclusion/exclusion criteria.[9]

- The result of a RCT is neither truth nor fact. A RCT is a single study, is dependent upon the strength of its methodology/analysis, and its result(s) must be weighed relative to prior data and clinical practicality.[11]

- RCTs may generate more questions than they answer, such that further study is required.[9,11]

Superiority trials test if the efficacy of an experimental medication is "superior" to that of a control group; the control may be placebo or an active, standard of care, treatment control. Superiority trials are **the gold standard study design for most fields of clinical study since they have the most concrete boundaries for detecting differences between evaluated groups**.

Non-Inferiority trials test if the efficacy of an experimental treatment (e.g., medication) is "not clinically inferior" to that of an active treatment control.[20] The **pre-defined non-inferiority margin (aka threshold) is based upon prior studies** (usually placebo controlled & sometimes only one study) **that tested the efficacy of the active treatment control. The non-inferiority margin is usually the smallest value considered to be clinically meaningful and usually <½ of the endpoint difference between the active treatment control and placebo.[20,34] Unless otherwise specified, the non-inferiority margin pertains solely to the primary endpoint of a study, rather than secondary, tertiary, or safety endpoints.**

- **Weaknesses of Non-inferiority trials:**
  - These are much more problematic in terms of reliability of results than are superiority trials since **weak internal validity is rewarded with bias towards non-inferiority**.[34]
    - There are multiple ways of calculating a NI boundary, some less accurate than others.[39]
    - Since the NI boundary is based upon a limited number of previous studies (sometimes only one), the NI boundary is not as concrete as a superiority boundary. For instance, the NI boundary may be based upon a study with a different patient population or region which limits its accuracy. Therefore,

even with using a 95% CI, there is little assurance of keeping type 1 error risk below 5%.[39]

- There is "no protection against blinded investigators' biasing the results toward a preconceived belief in non-inferiority by assigning similar ratings to the treatment responses of all patients."[30]

- "Discontinuations can obscure a true treatment effect."[30]

- **Analysis**

  - For non-inferiority trials, ITT analysis (see pages 166-168) often leads to smaller effect sizes and, therefore, tends to bias towards no difference between the evaluated groups.[30,34] This "could make a truly inferior treatment appear to be non-inferior."[30,34]

  - Per-protocol analysis (see page 169) could bias the results either towards or away from no difference between the evaluated groups.[30,34]

  - **Therefore non-inferiority trials should be analyzed using both ITT and Per-protocol analyses, and ONLY if BOTH support non-inferiority are the results considered conclusive.**[30]

Equivalence trials test if the efficacy of an experimental treatment (e.g., medication) is "sufficiently similar" to that of an active treatment control, to "justify use" of the experimental treatment.[20] **Pre-defined equivalence margins (aka thresholds) are based upon prior studies** (usually placebo controlled & sometimes only one study) **that tested the efficacy of the active treatment control. Unless otherwise specified, equivalence margins pertain solely to the primary endpoint of a study, rather than secondary, tertiary, or safety endpoints.**

- **Weaknesses of Equivalence trials:**

  - Just as with non-inferiority trials, equivalence trials are much more problematic in terms of reliability of results than are superiority trials since weak internal validity is rewarded with bias towards equivalence.[34,40]

    - Equivalence boundaries are not as concrete as superiority boundaries since they are based upon a limited number of previous trials (sometimes only one), so even with using a 95% CI, there is little assurance of keeping type 1 error risk below 5%.[39]

    - **Equivalence trials should be analyzed using both ITT and Per-protocol analyses,** (see pages 166-169) **and ONLY if BOTH support equivalence are the results considered conclusive.**[30,40]

- **Analysis**

    - For equivalence trials, ITT analysis (see pages 166-168) often leads to smaller effect sizes and, therefore, tends to bias towards no difference between the evaluated groups.[30,34,40] This "could make a truly inferior treatment appear to be equivalent"[30,34,40]

    - Per-protocol analysis (see page 169) could bias the results either towards or away from no difference between the evaluated groups.[30,34,40]

    - **Therefore <u>equivalence trials should be analyzed using both ITT and Per-protocol analyses, and ONLY if BOTH support equivalence are the results considered conclusive.</u>**[30,40]

Large simple trials (LSTs) are very large, multi-center, long-term trials with very broad inclusion criteria that study long term safety/efficacy of interventions under real word circumstances.

Study Questions: (Most of the following questions were provided by Melanie Pound, PharmD, BCPS)

74. A retrospective study produces correlation/regression analysis between a high sodium intake (>2.4 grams/day) and Hypertension reporting an r = 0.65.What is the most likely reason the relationship between HTN and high sodium intake is imperfect?
    a. Bias
    b. Confounding
    c. Carryover effect
    d. Cross-over design
    e. Both "a" and "b" are correct

75. A study of the effects of bupropion versus nicotine patches versus nicotine gum on smoking cessation rates is being developed in a parallel, randomized trial. The primary endpoint is the proportion of subjects that successfully quit smoking at 3 months. The investigators plan to include 450 subjects (150 in each arm) to reach statistical significance based upon a beta of 0.20 and alpha of 0.05.Which of the following is a potential benefit of utilizing a parallel trial design in the above study as compared to a cross-over design?
    a. Parallel trials have less inter-patient variability than cross-over trials.
    b. Parallel trials allow for a smaller sample size than cross-over trials.
    c. Parallel trials are more appropriate for this trial (smoking cessation treatment evaluation) than cross-over trials.
    d. There is no advantage to utilizing a parallel design with this study. A cross-over design would be most cost effective and efficient.

76. An investigator wishes to determine, "Which antibiotic— Camelcycline (new agent similar to tigecycline) or imipenem/vancomycin—will be more effective in treating complicated intra-abdominal infections?" To address this question, which of the following would be the BEST type of trial design?
    a. Randomized controlled trial
    b. Meta-analysis
    c. Prospective cohort
    d. Case-control study
    e. Case report

77. A cohort study evaluating the effect of troponin I levels in heart failure patients found that troponin levels ≥ 0.04 ng/mL was associated with increased mortality. All of the following are descriptors of this study design EXCEPT:
    a. Experimental
    b. Also known as an outcome study
    c. May be retrospective or prospective
    d. Good design for studying frequent outcomes or diseases
    e. All of the above describe a cohort study

78. A researcher wants to examine the risk of a rare side effect, hemorrhagic stroke. What is the best type of study design to utilize?
    a. Case-control study
    b. Retrospective cohort study
    c. Prospective cohort study
    d. Randomized controlled trial
    e. Meta-analysis

79. A researcher was interested in examining the association between post-menopausal HRT and development of heart disease. All women who were characterized as newly post-menopausal were approached regarding their interest in participating in the study by answering a questionnaire annually regarding their medication use and medical conditions. Of the 16,168 women who provided consent, the average length of follow-up was 12.5 years (range 6-16 years). Which of the following best describes the study design?
    a. Case-control study
    b. Prospective cohort study (truly prospective)
    c. Retrospective cohort study
    d. Randomized controlled trial
    e. Prospective cohort study (retrospective in nature)

80. An investigator wishes to study a new drug, Camelazil, for the treatment of hypertension in patients with diabetes. What study design would be best for determining causality in this particular study?
    a. A case-control study
    b. A prospective cohort study
    c. A prospective, randomized, placebo-controlled trial
    d. A prospective, randomized, standard-of-care comparison trial
    e. A meta-analysis

(for the next 2 questions)

81. An investigator wants to evaluate possible causes for a very rare type of exposure which may be linked to increases in A1c. Which of the following study designs is the most efficient, ethical, and objective to utilize in this situation?
    a. Randomized, controlled trial
    b. Cohort study
    c. Case-control study
    d. Case report series

82. What is an associated weakness with this study design?
    a. The Hawthorne Effect
    b. Difficulty balancing desired data collection and ethics
    c. Requires larger sample sizes than most other designs
    d. Cannot compute incidence
    e. Although confounding is not likely, bias is problematic with this design.

83. Which of the following would have the most power to detect clinically and statistically meaningful differences?
    a. RTC evaluating a new medication versus standard of care therapy and the combined primary endpoint of MI, stroke, or death.
    b. RTC evaluating a new medication versus standard of care therapy and the combined primary endpoint of MI or death.
    c. Retrospective Cohort evaluating a medication versus standard of care therapy and the combined primary endpoint of MI, stroke, PVD, HF, or death.
    d. Case Control study evaluating a medication versus standard of care therapy and the combined primary endpoint of MI, stroke, PVD, HF, DM, or death.

84. A researcher wants to evaluate the risk of cardiovascular disease and the association with asbestos exposure. The patients will be identified based on their exposure to asbestos. What is the best type of study design for evaluating this risk while minimizing bias and confounding?
    a. Prospective cohort
    b. Randomized, controlled trial
    c. Retrospective cohort
    d. Case-control trial

85. A researcher wants to evaluate the risk of a jaw osteonecrosis and the association with bisphosphonate use as well as other possible risk factors. The patients were identified by the radiologists who confirmed the x-ray findings. Which of the following is the best type of trial design for the study?
    a. Randomized, controlled trial
    b. Prospective cohort
    c. Case-control study
    d. Case report

Answers to Study Questions:

74. e - Retrospective designs are subject to bias and confounding. Also, there are confounding variables (e.g., genetics, physical inactivity, stress, pain, etc.) which prevent a perfect relationship between hypertension and high sodium intake.

75. c - It would be unethical to have smokers who quit during the first part of the trial to start smoking again for the latter part(s) of the cross-over trial, so a parallel trial would be beneficial with this scenario. Cross-over trials allow for smaller sample sizes and have less inter-patient variability than parallel trials since patients serve as their own controls.

76. a - A well performed RCT is the most effective way to establish causality: in this case, antibiotic "causing" clearing an infection. The relative strength of causality for MA or systematic review is controversial, the MA would have to include only well conducted RCTs for some to consider them to be stronger than RCTs for establishing causality. Camelcycline is a new drug, so there would not likely be several well conducted RCTs to include in the MA. Cohorts are stronger than case-control studies which are stronger than case reports, but all of these are weaker than a well conducted RCT.

77. a

78. a - Since patients are identified based upon a rare outcome, hemorrhagic stroke, a case-control is the best study design to use.

79. b - Since patients were identified based upon exposure (being newly post-menopausal – questionnaire to identify HRT), this was a cohort design. Since data regarding the exposure (being newly post-menopausal – questionnaire to identify HRT) and the outcome (heart disease), were collected in the present or future, this was a truly prospective cohort. If the exposure had taken place in the past and the outcome in the future, this would be a prospective cohort design that is retrospective in nature. If both the exposure and outcome had occurred in the past, this would be a retrospective cohort. If the patients had been randomized to either receive or not receive HRT, it would have been a RCT. If patients had been identified based upon outcome (heart disease), it would have been a case-control design.

80. d - A well performed RCT is the most effective way to establish causality: in this case treating hypertension in patients with diabetes. Since we already have strong outcomes data for several agents in treating hypertension in diabetes patients, it would be unethical to use a placebo-control. Therefore, a standard treatment control must be used. The relative strength of causality for MA or systematic review is controversial, the meta-analysis would have to include only well conducted RCTs for some to consider them to be stronger than RCTs for establishing causality. Camelazil is a new drug, so there would not likely be several well conducted RCTs to include in the MA. Case control studies are weak with regard to establishing causality.

81. b - Since the exposure is rare, it would be most efficient to identify patients based upon this rare exposure. Therefore, a cohort is the best design to utilize. It would be unethical to perform a RCT since we would have to intentionally expose patients to something that we currently hypothesize may increase risk for rise in A1c, and therefore, the likelihood of developing diabetes. Case-control would be very inefficient since this design identifies patients based upon outcome (rise in A1c in this case) and would not likely identify the rare exposure the investigators are trying to evaluate. Case report series is weaker than any of these designs with regard to helping establish causality.

82. a

83. a - For establishing causality, RCTs are stronger than cohorts are stronger than case-control studies. Combined endpoints increase incidence because more outcomes lead to increased incidence. Therefore, there's more power to detect differences between groups when these differences truly exist.

84. a - Since patients are identified based on exposure (or risk factor, asbestos exposure), this is a cohort study; also CV disease is a frequent disease (endpoint, outcome). Prospective cohorts are stronger than retrospective cohorts for minimizing bias and confounding. RCT is not an option since it would be unethical to purposefully expose patients to asbestos. This is not a case-control study since patients are not identified based upon an endpoint (or outcome).

85. c - Since patients are identified based on disease (x-ray confirmed osteonecrosis), this is a case-control design. A RCT would be impractical since the findings may not show up for years after exposure. A cohort may be used to confirm results of this case-control study, but may be impractical since the findings may not show up for years after exposure. Also bisphosphonates are widely used and cohorts usually focus on rare exposures. A case report would only be descriptive.

Part 9: Risk Calculations

Risk calculations estimate the magnitude of association between exposure and outcome.[9,11] These effect measurers are mainly used for nominal outcomes, but in rare cases may be applied to ordinal outcomes. The following calculations for cohort and RCT are the same, but nomenclature is different. For a cohort study, the exposed group is referred to as such. For a RCT, the exposed group may be referred to as the experimental, treatment, or interventional group. For a cohort study, the unexposed group is referred to as such. For a RCT, the unexposed group is referred to as the control group. For the following examples, the subscript "E" will refer to the exposed or experimental (treatment, interventional) group and the subscript "C" will refer to the unexposed or control group.

- **Absolute risk (AR) is simply another term for incidence**: the number of ***new cases*** that occur during a specified time period divided by the number of subjects initially followed to detect an outcome of interest.[3]

  $$AR = \frac{\text{number who develop outcome during a specified time period}}{\text{number available to develop outcome at the beginning of the study}}$$

- **Absolute risk reduction (ARR)** is a measure of the absolute incidence differences in the event rate between the studied groups. Absolute differences are more meaningful than relative differences in outcomes when evaluating clinical studies.[27] When outcomes are worse for the experimental group, the absolute risk difference is termed absolute risk increase (ARI).

  $$\text{ARR (or ARI)} = AR_C - AR_E$$

- **Numbers-needed-to-treat (NNT) is the** "reciprocal of the absolute risk reduction(ARR)"[9,15] When outcomes are better for the experimental group, there is an absolute risk reduction (ARR) and this calculation is referred to as numbers needed to treat (NNT).

  $$NNT = \frac{1}{ARR}$$

  - When outcomes are worse for the experimental group, there is an absolute risk increase (ARI) and this calculation is referred to as numbers-needed-to-harm (NNH) .

  $$NNH = \frac{1}{ARI}$$

- Generally, **absolute differences (ARR and ARI) will be larger in placebo control trials** than for active treatment control trials. **Therefore, NNT and NNH will generally be much smaller for placebo control trials** than for active treatment control trials.

- **NNT and NNH** help in understanding the magnitude of an intervention's effectiveness and **should always be calculated when evaluating medical literature** in preference to relative risk (RR) or hazards ratio (HR) **since NNT and NNH are more indicative of the true clinical impact on patient populations**.[9]

- Although rarely seen, "confidence intervals may be calculated for NNT and NNH."[27]

- A weakness of these is that they "assume baseline risk is the same for all patients or that it is unrelated to relative risk."[9,15]

- **NNT and NNH are sometimes presented as "person-years-needed-to-treat (or harm)"**. This is especially the case for meta-analyses since length of follow-up of included studies differ; one study may have lasted 3 years while another may have lasted 7 years and another may have lasted 10 years. Although this is beneficial in helping aggregate data, a weakness is that it assumes a constant effect over time.

    - 3 persons x 10 years = 30 person-years

    - 6 persons x 7 years = 42 person-years

    - 10 persons x 3 years = 30 person-years

- **Relative risk (RR) – aka rate ratio, risk ratio) compares the AR (incidence) of the experimental group to that of the control group**.[9] It is simply a ratio of the AR for the experimental or exposed group to the AR of the control or unexposed group. RR is sometimes called risk ratio, rate ratio, or incidence rate ratio.

$$RR = \frac{AR_E}{AR_C}$$

- **Relative risk differences are sometimes presented in studies and these estimate the percentage of baseline risk that is changed between the exposed or experimental group and the unexposed or control group.[15] The relative risk difference is termed relative risk reduction (RRR) when risk is decreased. The relative risk difference is termed relative risk increase (RRI) when risk is increased. RRR and RRI can be calculated in two different ways.**

  RRR (or RRI) = 1 – RR

  or…

  $$\text{RRR (or RRI)} = \frac{\text{ARR (or ARI)}}{\text{AR}_C}$$

- **Hazard Ratio (HR)** is used with Cox Proportion Hazards Regression analysis. It is used when a study is evaluating the length of time required for an outcome of interest to occur.[35] HR is often used similarly to RR, and is a reasonable estimate of RR as long as adequate data are collected and outcome incidence is <15%.[35,42] However, whereas RR only represents the probability of having an event between the beginning and end of a study, HR can represent the probability of having an event during a certain time interval between the beginning and end of the study.[27]

- **Odds Ratio (OR)** is mainly used in case-control studies as an estimate of RR since incidence cannot be calculated. Estimation accuracy decreases as outcome or disease incidence increases. However, OR is fairly accurate as long as disease incidence is <15% which is usually the case since case-control studies evaluate potential risk factors for rare diseases.[35] In addition, OR is sometimes reported for RCTs utilizing logistic or multivariate regression analysis simply because these analyses automatically calculate OR. They do so because regression analysis is utilized to adjust for confounding and adjustments are easier to perform with OR than with RR.[32]

  - OR is presented differently for case-control studies than for RCTs.

    - For RCTs, OR is presented in same way as RR.

      - For example, in a RCT evaluating an association of an intervention and death rate, an OR of 0.75 would be reported as: patients receiving the intervention were 25% less likely, or 75% as likely, to have died than controls.

- Since case-control studies identify patients based upon disease rather than intervention, OR is presented differently than for a RCT; it compares the odds that a case was exposed to a risk factor, to the odds that a control was exposed to a risk factor.[11]
    - For example, in a case-control study evaluating an association of a rare type of cancer and exposure to pesticides, an OR of 1.5 would be reported as: cases (those with the rare cancer) were 50% more likely, or 1 ½ times as likely, to have been exposed to pesticides than controls.

- 95% CIs should always be provided for RR, OR, and HR.

Relative Risk Example 1:

A RCT reported rates of hospitalization 5 years after initiation of either metoprolol or the placebo control. Average follow-up was 3 years. In the metoprolol group, 400 out of the 2010 patients were hospitalized, compared to 675 out of 2000 receiving placebo.

		ENDPOINT		
		+ **Hospitalized**	- **Not hospitalized**	
INTERVENTION	+ Metoprolol **Experimental group**	A = 400 # of experimental pts w/ outcome of interest	B = 1610 # of experimental pts w/out outcome of interest	400 +1610 2010
	- Placebo **Control group**	C = 675 # of control pts w/ outcome of interest	D = 1325 # of control pts w/out outcome of interest	675 + 1325 2000

AR_C (or incidence) for the Control Group =

$$\frac{\text{number who developed the outcome during a specified time period (C)}}{\text{number available to develop the outcome at the beginning of the study (C+D)}}$$

$AR_C = 675 / (675 + 1325) = 675 / 2000 = 0.3375 =$ 34% risk of hospitalization in 3 years for the control group

AR_E (or incidence) for the Experimental Group =

$$\frac{\text{number who developed the outcome during a specified time period (A)}}{\text{number available to develop the outcome at the beginning of the study (A+B)}}$$

$AR_E = 400 / (400 + 1610) = 400 / 2010 = 0.199 =$ 20% risk of hospitalization in 3 years for the experimental (interventional) group

$ARR = AR_C - AR_E = 34\% - 20\% = 14\%$ (or $0.34 - 0.20 = 0.14$)

$$NNT = \frac{1}{ARR} = \frac{1}{0.14} = 7.14$$

So one can report NNT as follows:

- Need to treat 7 or 8 patients for 3 years to prevent 1 hospitalization

$$RR = \frac{AR_E}{AR_C} = \frac{\frac{A}{(A+B)}}{\frac{C}{(C+D)}} = \frac{0.20}{0.34} = 0.59$$

So pts in the experimental group were 0.59 times, or 59% **as** Likely to have been hospitalized over 3 years, relative to the control group

RRR: 2 ways to calculate RRR

- RRR = 1 – RR = 1 – 0.59 = 0.41

or…

- $RRR = \frac{ARR}{AR_C} = \frac{0.34 - 0.20}{0.34} = \frac{0.14}{0.34} = 0.41$

So pts in the experimental group were 41% **less** likely to have been hospitalized over 3 years, relative to those in the control group

These same calculations are used for a **Cohort Study Design**, except that the Experimental group would be referred to as the Exposed group and the Control Group would be referred to as the Non-exposed group.

		ENDPOINT		
		+ **Hospitalized**	- **Not hospitalized**	
EXPOSURE	+ Metoprolol **Exposed group**	A = 400 # of exposed pts w/ endpoint of interest	B = 1610 # of exposed pts w/out endpoint of interest	400 +1610 = 2010
	- Placebo **Non-exposed group**	C = 675 # of non-exposed pts w/ endpoint of interest	D = 1325 # of non-exposed pts w/out endpoint of interest	675 + 1325 = 2000

Relative Risk Example 2 is the opposite scenario:

A RCT reported rates of hospitalization 5 years after initiation of either metoprolol or the placebo control. Average follow up was 3 years. In the metoprolol group, 675 out of the 2010 patients were hospitalized, compared to 400 out of the 2000 receiving placebo.

		ENDPOINT		
		+ Hospitalized	**- Not hospitalized**	
INTERVENTION	+ Metoprolol **Experimental group**	A = 675 # of experimental pts w/ outcome of interest	B = 1335 # of experimental pts w/out outcome of interest	675 +1335 2010
	- Placebo **Control group**	C = 400 # of control pts w/ outcome of interest	D = 1600 # of control pts w/out outcome of interest	400 + 1600 2000

AR_C (or incidence) for the Control Group =

$$\frac{\text{number who developed the outcome during a specified time period (C)}}{\text{number available to develop the outcome at the beginning of the study(C+D)}}$$

$AR_C = 400 / (400 + 1600) = 400 / 2000 = 0.20 =$ 20% risk of hospitalization in 3 years for the control group

AR_E (or incidence) for the Experimental Group =

$$\frac{\text{number who developed the outcome during a specified time period (A)}}{\text{number available to develop the outcome at the beginning of the study (A+B)}}$$

$AR_E = 675 / (675 + 1335) = 675 / 2010 = 0.336 =$ 34% risk of hospitalization in 3 years for the experimental (interventional) group

ARI (absolute risk increase) = $AR_C - AR_E$ = 20% - 34% = ¯14% (or 0.20 - 0.34 = ¯0.14)

= 14% ARI

NNH (numbers needed to harm) = $\frac{1}{ARI}$ = $\frac{1}{0.14}$ = 7.14

So one can report NNH as follows:

- Need to treat 7 or 8 patients for 3 years to cause 1 hospitalization.

$$RR = \frac{AR_E}{AR_C} = \frac{\frac{A}{(A + B)}}{\frac{C}{(C + D)}} = \frac{0.34}{0.20} = 1.70$$

So pts in the experimental group were 1.7 times as likely to have been hospitalized over 3 years, relative to those in the control group.

RRI (relative risk increase): 2 ways to calculate RRI

- RRI = 1 – RR = 1 – 1.70 = 0.70 = 70% RRI

Or…

- $RRI = \frac{ARI}{AR_C} = \frac{0.14}{0.20}$ = 0.70 = 70% RRI

  So pts in the experimental group were 70% **more** likely to have been hospitalized over 3 years, relative to those in the control group.

The same calculations could be used for a **Cohort Study Design**, except the Experimental group would be referred to as the Exposed group and the Control Group would be referred to as the Non-exposed group.

		ENDPOINT		
		+ Hospitalized	**- Not hospitalized**	
EXPOSURE	+ Metoprolol **Exposed group**	A = 675 # of exposed pts w/ endpoint of interest	B = 1335 # of exposed pts w/out endpoint of interest	675 +1335 2010
	- Placebo **Non-exposed group**	C = 400 # of non-exposed pts w/ endpoint of interest	D = 1600 # of non-exposed pts w/out endpoint of interest	400 + 1600 2000

Now let's use the same examples to calculate OR for a case-control study scenario.

Odds Ratio Example 1:

A case-control study identified hospitalized patients and determined the odds of whether or not these patients were exposed to metoprolol.

400 patients were hospitalized out of 2010 patients who had been exposed to metoprolol.

675 patients were hospitalized out of 2000 patients who were not exposed to metoprolol.

Note:

- In a case-control study, patients are identified based upon presence or absence of a particular disease or endpoint (hospitalization in this scenario), rather than exposure (as with the cohort study design).
- A case-control study would examine multiple possible exposures, but for simplicity, this example will only focus on metoprolol.
- As discussed earlier, since incidence cannot be calculated for case-control studies, RR is approximated through calculating OR.

<table>
<tr><td colspan="2"></td><td colspan="2">ENDPOINT</td><td></td></tr>
<tr><td colspan="2"></td><td>+
Hospitalized
CASES</td><td>-
Not hospitalized
CONTROLS</td><td></td></tr>
<tr><td rowspan="2">EXPOSURE</td><td>+
Metoprolol</td><td>A = 400
# of cases exposed to the risk factor</td><td>B = 1610
# of controls exposed to the risk factor</td><td>400
+1610
2010</td></tr>
<tr><td>-
No Metoprolol</td><td>C = 675
# of cases not exposed to risk factor</td><td>D = 1325
# of controls not exposed to the risk factor</td><td>675
+ 1325
2000</td></tr>
<tr><td colspan="2"></td><td>1075
Total Cases</td><td>2935
Total Controls</td><td></td></tr>
</table>

OR (odds ratio) = $\dfrac{A/C}{B/D}$ which also = $\dfrac{AD}{BC}$

Here is how this equation was formulated:

$$\frac{\dfrac{A/(A+C)}{C/(A+C)}}{\dfrac{B/(B+D)}{D/(B+D)}} = \frac{\dfrac{A/(A+\not{C})}{C/(\not{A}+C)}}{\dfrac{B/(B+\not{D})}{D/(\not{B}+D)}} = \frac{A/C}{B/D}$$

Through cross-multiplication one can also see that

$$\frac{A/C}{B/D} = \frac{AD}{BC}$$

Since $\dfrac{A/C}{B/D}$ also = A/C x D/B

If one multiplies by D/D, then $\dfrac{A}{C} \times \dfrac{\not{D}}{B} \times \dfrac{D}{\not{D}} = \dfrac{AD}{BC}$

One will get the same answer regardless of how one decides to calculate OR

$$\frac{A/C}{B/D} = \frac{400 / 675}{1610 / 1325} = \frac{0.593}{1.215} = 0.49$$

$$\frac{AD}{BC} = \frac{400 \times 1325}{1610 \times 675} = \frac{530000}{1086750} = 0.49$$

For this case-control study scenario, this can be presented in two ways:

- Hospitalized patients were 49% **as** likely to have been exposed to metoprolol...
- Or, since 1-0.49 = 0.51, hospitalized patients were 51% **less** likely to have received metoprolol.

Odds Ratio Example 2 is the opposite scenario:

A case-control study identified hospitalized patients and determined the odds of whether or not patients were exposed to metoprolol.

675 patients were hospitalized out of 2010 patients who had been exposed to metoprolol.

400 patients were hospitalized out of 2000 patients who were not exposed to metoprolol.

Note:

- In a case-control study, patients are identified based upon presence or absence of a particular disease or endpoint (hospitalization in this scenario), rather than exposure (as with the cohort study design).
- A case-control study would examine multiple possible exposures, but for simplicity, this example will only focus on metoprolol.
- As discussed earlier, since incidence cannot be calculated for case-control studies, RR is approximated through calculating OR.

<table>
<tr><td></td><td></td><td colspan="2">ENDPOINT</td><td></td></tr>
<tr><td></td><td></td><td>+
Hospitalized
CASES</td><td>-
Not hospitalized
CONTROLS</td><td></td></tr>
<tr><td rowspan="2">EXPOSURE</td><td>+
Metoprolol</td><td>A = 675
# of cases exposed to the risk factor</td><td>B = 1335
# of controls exposed to the risk factor</td><td>675
+1335
2010</td></tr>
<tr><td>-
No Metoprolol</td><td>C = 400
# of cases not exposed to risk factor</td><td>D = 1600
# of controls not exposed to the risk factor</td><td>400
+ 1600
2000</td></tr>
<tr><td></td><td></td><td>1075
Total Cases</td><td>2935
Total Controls</td><td></td></tr>
</table>

OR (odds ratio) = $\frac{A/C}{B/D}$ which also = $\frac{AD}{BC}$

One will get the same answer regardless of how one decides to calculate OR

$$\frac{A/C}{B/D} = \frac{675 / 400}{1335 / 1600} = \frac{1.6875}{0.8344} = 2.02$$

$$\frac{AD}{BC} = \frac{675 \times 1600}{1335 \times 400} = \frac{1080000}{534000} = 2.02$$

For this case-control study scenario, this can be presented in two ways:

- Hospitalized patients were approximately **twice as likely** to have been exposed to metoprolol…
- or, since 1 - 2.02 = $^{-}$1.02, hospitalized patients were 102% more likely to have been exposed to metoprolol.

Note concerning change in incidence's effect on estimation of Relative Risk

Remember that OR provides a good estimate of RR as long as the **incidence** of disease is low and the cases and controls are representative of the population being studied. But in these 2 examples **incidence was very high** relative to what one would expect to see in a case-control study since case-control designs are usually used for rare outcomes. So the ORs did not appear to be very accurate. For RR and OR examples 1 the calculated values were 0.59 and 0.49, respectively. For RR and OR examples 2 the calculated values were 1.70 and 2.02, respectively. I just wanted to work through the examples using the same numbers so that you would have a comparison to work with in the future.

Study Questions: (Most of the following questions were provided by Melanie Pound, PharmD, BCPS)

86. What is the best way to describe the results of this cohort study which lasted an average of 9 months?

	# of Fudge-eaters (n=60)	# of non-Fudge-eaters (n=65)
Hypertriglyceridemia	27	15

   a. The calculated RR is 1.95
   b. The calculated OR is 2.73
   c. Fudge-eaters are 95% more likely to get hypertriglyceridemia compared with non-fudge-eaters
   d. Fudge-eaters are 200% more likely to get hypertriglyceridemia compared with non-fudge-eaters
   e. Only "a" and "c" are correct answers

87. An investigator wants to evaluate possible causes for a very rare type of exposure which may be linked to increases in A1c. Which of the following describes the most desirable to use when comparing the groups in this study?
   a. odds ratio
   b. relative risk
   c. numbers needed to treat
   d. numbers needed to harm

88. The results from a case-control study evaluating the association of QT prolongation with dofetilide revealed the following:

	QT prolongation	No QT prolongation
Dofetilide	123	177
No dofetilide	65	235

What can be concluded about these results?
   a. Patients with QT prolongation were 251% more likely to have taken dofetilide.
   b. Patients taking dofetilide are 2.51 times as likely to experience QT prolongation relative to patients not taking dofetilide.
   c. The calculated RR is 1.89.
   d. The calculated OR is 2.51.
   e. Patients taking dofetilide are 1.89 times as likely to experience QT prolongation relative to patients not taking dofetilide.

89. Investigators wish to study the association between aluminum exposure and of risk of Alzheimer's. The results from this 30 year cohort study are listed below:

	Aluminum (n=55)	No aluminum(n=62)
Alzheimer's	35	17

Which of the following states is correct regarding the results?

a. Persons exposed to aluminum are 360% more likely to develop Alzheimer's compared with non-exposed persons.
b. Persons exposed to aluminum are 130% more likely to develop Alzheimer's compared with non-exposed persons.
c. The calculated OR is 2.3
d. The calculated RR is 2.3
e. Both "b" and "d" are correct answers

(for the next 4 questions)

The AVERROES trial is a superiority trial that studied the effects of apixaban versus aspirin in atrial fibrillation patients unable to take vitamin K antagonists for the prevention of stroke. The primary endpoint was the occurrence of stroke or systemic embolism. The study period was 1.1 years and the results are presented below:

	Apix (n=2808)	Aspirin (n=2791)	HR (95%CI)
Primary endpt	51	113	0.45 (0.32 – 0.62)
Sec endpts			
CVA or death	143	223	0.64 (0.51 - 0.78)
Ischemic CVA	35	93	0.37 (0.25 - 0.55)
Hemorrhagic CVA	6	9	0.67 (0.24 – 1.88)
MI	24	28	0.86 (0.5 – 1.48)
All deaths (AD)	111	140	0.79 (0.62 – 1.02)
Major bleeding	44	39	1.13 (0.74 – 1.75)

90. Based on the results above, what can NOT be concluded about the primary endpoint with regards to apixaban versus aspirin?

a. The unadjusted estimated relative risk is 0.45.
b. The estimated relative risk reduction is 55%.
c. The absolute risk reduction is 2.93%.
d. The number needed to treat is 45 patients for 1.1 yrs.

91. Which of the following is FALSE concerning the secondary endpoints with regards to apixaban versus aspirin?

a. The NNT to prevent 1 ischemic stroke with apixaban for 1.1 years is 48.
b. If treating 589 patients with aspirin for 1.1 years, 1 patient may experience a major bleed compared with the apixiban group.
c. The unadjusted RR for MI is 0.85.
d. Although fewer patients died in the apixaban group, there is no statistically significant difference from the aspirin group.

92. If this trial were a non-inferiority trial, and the non-inferiority margin for all endpoints were prespecified at 1.5, which of the following outcome(s) would be considered non-inferior?
    a. MI and major bleed
    b. All deaths and hemorrhagic CVA
    c. MI and all deaths
    d. Hemorrhagic CVA and major bleed

93. If this trial were a non-inferiority trial, and the non-inferiority margin for all endpoints were prespecified at 1.48, which of the following outcome(s) would be considered non-inferior?
    a. MI and major bleed
    b. All deaths and hemorrhagic CVA
    c. MI and all deaths
    d. All deaths

Answers to Study Questions:

86. e - RR should be used for cohort studies. OR is mainly used for case-control studies. AR_E (fudge eaters) = 27/60 = 0.45 or 45%, AR_C (control-non-fudge eaters) = 15/65 = 0.23 or 23%; ARI = AR_C - AR_E = 0.23-0.45 = 0.22 or 22%, NNH= 1/0.22 = 4.5, so 5 patients over 9 months. In other words, 5 patients would have to eat fudge over an average of 9 months to cause one of the patients to develop hypertriglyceridemia. RR=0.45/0.23 = 1.95. The results could be reported as fudge eaters were 1.95 times as likely to develop hypertriglyceridemia as non-fudge eaters. Since RRI = 1-RR = 1-1.95 = $^{-}0.95$, another way of explaining the results would be that fudge eaters were 95% more likely to develop hypertriglyceridemia as non-fudge eaters.

87. b - Since outcomes for a rare exposure will be evaluated, a cohort study which identifies patients based upon the rare exposure would be most appropriate. RR should be used for cohort studies.

88. d - OR is used for case-control studies. For this example, the OR is (A/C)/(B/D) or AD/BC = {[(123)(235)/[(177)(65)]} = 2.51, which means that patients identified as having QT interval prolongation (cases) were 2.5 times as likely to have been exposed to dofetilide as those who did not have QT interval prolongation (controls). Since 1 - 2.5 = $^{-}1.5$, another way of explaining these results would be that patients identified as having QT interval prolongation (cases) were 1.5 times more likely to have been exposed to dofetilide as those who did not have QT interval prolongation (controls).

89. e - RR is used for cohort studies. AR_E (aluminum exposure) = 35/55 = 0.64 or 64%, AR_C (control-no aluminum exposure) = 17/62 = 0.27 or 27%; ARI = AR_C - AR_E = 0.27-0.64 = 0.37 or 37%, NNH= 1/0.37 = 2.7, so 3 patients over 30 years. In other words, 3 patients would have to be exposed to aluminum over an average of 30 years to cause one of the patients to develop Alzheimer's. RR=0.64/0.27 = 2.3. The results could be reported as those exposed to aluminum were 2.3 times as likely to develop Alzheimer's as those not exposed to aluminum. Since RRI = 1-RR = 1-2.3 = $^{-}1.3$, another way of explaining the results would be that those exposed to aluminum were 130% more likely to develop Alzheimer's as those not exposed to aluminum.

90. c - For the primary endpoint, AR_E (experimental group-apixaban) = 0.01816 = 1.816%, AR_C (control-ASA) = 0.04049 = 4.049%; ARR = AR_C - AR_E = 0.0223 = 2.23%, NNT= 1/0.0223 = 44.8 = 45 patients over an average of 1.1 years. In other words, 45 patients would have to be treated with apixaban rather than aspirin over an average of 1.1 years (approximately 1 year) to prevent one primary endpoint. RR=1.816/4.049 = 0.45. The results could be reported as those treated with apixaban were 0.45 times as likely to experience a primary endpoint as those taking aspirin. Since RRR = 1-RR = 1-0.45 = 0.55, another way of explaining the results would be that those taking apixaban were 55% less likely to have experienced a primary endpoint than those taking aspirin.

91. b - NNT and NNH are meaningless when results are not significant, which is why answer b is incorrect. Answers a, c, and d are all true. Have to work through the raw numbers to calculate an unadjusted RR for MI of 0.85.

92. c - In order for these outcomes to be non-inferior, the CI must NOT include 1.5. Of the options listed, ONLY MI and AD confidence intervals do NOT include 1.5. Since the primary endpoint, CVA or death, and ischemic CVA exclude 1, these are reported as being superior rather than non-inferior.

93. d - In order for these outcomes to be non-inferior, the CI must NOT include 1.48. Of the options listed, ONLY "all deaths" falls below and does not include 1.48.

Part 10: Various Types of Analyses

- **Including:**
  - **Intention-to-treat (ITT) analysis**
  - **Modified ITT analysis**
  - **As-treated analysis**
  - **Per-protocol analysis**
  - **Post-study (aka post-hoc) analysis**
  - **Interim analysis**
  - **Multiple analyses**
  - **Subgroup analysis**
  - **Survival analysis**
  - **Meta-analysis (MA)**

- **Intention-to-treat (ITT)** analysis compares outcomes between groups based upon subjects' initial assignment.[9]

  - For example, in a trial evaluating fluconazole vs amphotericin B, a patient assigned to receive fluconazole, but accidentally receiving amphotericin B, will be analyzed as having received fluconazole.

  - This makes finding a difference between interventions difficult and is why ITT is considered the most conservative treatment effect estimate. However, ITT's benefit is that it closely approximates interventions' effectiveness for the real-world, clinical setting.[9,15]

- ITT maintains power since data for all randomized subjects are analyzed: "once randomized always analyzed."[15,17]

- For superiority trials, ITT generally provides a better estimate or approximation of how an intervention will perform in a real world setting.[15]

- For non-inferiority and equivalence trials, ITT analysis often leads to smaller effect sizes and, therefore, tends to bias against finding a difference between the evaluated groups.[30,34] This "could make a truly inferior treatment appear non-inferior or equivalent."[30,34] This is why non-inferiority and equivalence trials should be analyzed using not only ITT, but also per protocol analysis, and "only if both support non-inferiority or equivalence is the trial considered positive."[30]

- Since some study subjects miss appointments, fail to have their scheduled lab work completed, or simply stop participation in trials before completion, ITT utilizes one of two methods for imputing missing data: 1) worst case scenario or 2) last observation carried forward (LOCF).[17, 31]

- Worst case scenario underestimates effect size.[9,15, 31]
    - For example: if the outcome being evaluated in the ITT trial is death, all patients missing at the end of the trial will be analyzed as having died.
    - As seen with this example, when the amount of missing data increases, outcomes for the studied interventions become more similar and power to detect true differences decreases.
- Last observation carried forward (LOCF) may over- or underestimate effect size.
    - Example of overestimating benefit: GI adverse effect data for COX-2 inhibitors are better at 6 months than at 12 months. So if LOCF is used, the COX-2 inhibitor data will look better for patients without data after 6 months because the 6 month data will be "carried forward" in place of the missing 12 month data.
    - Example of underestimating benefit: CV data for ACEIs are better at 2 years than at 6 months. So if LOCF is used, the ACEI data will look worse for patients without data after 6 months because the 6 month data will be "carried forward" in place of the missing 2 year data.

- Some trials claim to be ITT, but are not. For example, an active treatment run-in phase with some trials helps investigators weed-out subjects who are non-compliant, have AEs, or are allergic to trial medications. An active treatment run-in phase is a pre-trial phase during which all potential study subjects receive the active experimental medication(s) prior to acceptance into the trial. Other issues with an active treatment run-in phase include:
    - Run-in phase with active drug
        - This is sometimes required to protect subjects from risks associated with untreated disease where it would be unethical to utilize a placebo control, even for a short period of time.
        - At other times it corrupts the intention of ITT.
            - It may be used to make AE profiles appear better for the experimental medication. For example, if subjects are dismissed from an ACEI trial after having experienced angioedema from the ACEI during the run-in phase, angioedema incidence data will be underestimated for that particular ACEI. This would also cause overestimation of adherence estimates.

- It may also negate blinding. For example, investigators may note hyperkalemia, elevated BUN, or SCr. Subjects who received active medication during the run-in phase and placebo during the trial may feel differently or recognize some other difference: cough, dizziness, lightheadedness, headache, edema, or weakness.

- A run-in phase with placebo may not affect blinding in some cases and is sometimes used to ensure patient adherence via pill counts

- **Modified ITT (mITT)**:

  - This is like ITT with the **exception** of allowing for the exclusion of certain subjects. For example, subjects who withdrew from the study prior to receiving one of the interventions being evaluated would be excluded and therefore, not included in the analysis. Another example would be subjects who only took one dose of study medication without having a follow-up visit would be excluded and therefore, not included in the analysis. Unfortunately, studies which claim to be ITT, but are actually mITT are quite common. However, in cases where exclusions are justified, mITT will provide a more accurate assessment of any differences between the interventions being evaluated.

  - mITT may **not** maintain power since data for some randomized subjects may not be analyzed.

  - As with ITT, worst-case-scenario or LOCF can be utilized for missing data in mITT trials.[17, 20, 31]

- **As-treated** analysis compares outcomes between groups based upon what subjects actually receive.[9,15]

  - For example, in a trial evaluating fluconazole vs amphotericin B, a patient assigned to receive fluconazole, but accidentally receiving amphotericin B, will be analyzed as having received amphotericin B.

  - This provides a better estimate of any true difference(s) between treatments than does ITT. However, since reality is that patients sometimes receive incorrect medications, as-treated is less accurate than ITT in approximating interventions' effectiveness for the real-world, clinical setting.[9,15,17]

  - As-treated maintains power since data for all randomized subjects are analyzed: "once randomized always analyzed."[15,17]

  - As with ITT and mITT, worst-case-scenario or LOCF can be utilized for missing data.[17, 20, 31]

- **Per-protocol** analysis does not follow the "once randomized always analyzed" methodology of ITT and as-treated analyses. With per-protocol, only data from subjects who are strictly adherent to the study's protocol are analyzed.[15]
    - For example, if taking 85% of study medication is a protocol requirement, a subject will be excluded from analysis if he/she takes 84% of the study medication.
    - This makes finding a difference between interventions easier as long as enough patients are compliant with the protocol to maintain power. It also provides a better estimate of any true difference(s) between treatments than do ITT, mITT, or as-treated analyses. However, since non-adherence is a reality, per-protocol is less accurate than ITT, mITT, or as-treated analyses in approximating interventions' effectiveness for the real-world, clinical setting.[9,15,17]
    - Since per-protocol data are so "clean", it is very useful in evaluating ADR data because it provides a clearer picture of the true ADRs.
- Since non-compliant patients are excluded from per-protocol analysis, there will be loss of power to detect any true differences between groups. Therefore, it is important to estimate how many subjects will be excluded from the final analysis so that extra subjects can be initially included in the trial to minimize the risk of a type 2 error (an "under-powered" trial).
    - For example, if investigators expect 70% of subjects to strictly follow the study protocol, this would mean they expect 30% to be non-adherent. If the power calculation required 123 patients in each group to reach 80% power to detect a 25% relative difference between the 2 groups....

$$\textbf{Sample size} = \frac{123}{(1 - 0.3)} = \frac{123}{0.7} = 175.7$$

176 patients would be needed in each group to reach 80% power to detect a 25% difference between the 2 groups.

- For non-inferiority and equivalence trials, "per protocol analysis could bias" either towards or against finding a statistically significant result.[30,34] This is why non-inferiority and equivalence trials should be analyzed using not only per-protocol analysis, but also ITT, and "only if both support non-inferiority or equivalence is the trial considered positive."[30]

- **Post-study (aka post-hoc)** analyses are appropriate in some cases and not in others.

  - **Appropriate post-hoc analyses**

    - ANOVA with ≥3 samples, χ^2 tests with matrices larger than 2x2, Kruskal-Wallis and Friedman tests all indicate if a difference exists between groups, but they will not indicate where this difference exists.[5,11] Various post-hoc tests are necessary to determine where any difference lies.[4] These post-hoc tests should only be performed if a statistically significant difference was detected. Doing otherwise would increase type 1 error risk.

  - **Inappropriate post-hoc analyses**

    - Un-planned, unwarranted post-hoc analyses can be quite misleading since sometimes investigators are simply manipulating data to support their own products or opinions. This is referred to as data-dredging.

    - This type of data collection is retrospective and therefore hypothesis generating. Also, the more a data set is manipulated and analyzed, the higher the risk for type 1 error.

- **Interim analyses** (aka **alpha spending functions**) help ensure patient safety and can occur multiple times for long studies. At prespecified study time points, safety and efficacy data are collected and reviewed to determine if one treatment is better or worse than another. Based upon preset statistically and clinically significant boundaries, a trial may be stopped early. Trials are generally stopped early to protect study participants, but may be stopped early for reasons as simple as lack of funding.

  - If investigators find a significant benefit from an investigational medication, it may be unethical to withhold this medication from the control group.

  - If investigators uncover a clinically meaningful adverse effect from a new medication, it would be unethical to continue subjecting trial participants to the medication since it may cause harm. For example, in one of the interim analyses of the ALLHAT trial, it was discovered that doxazosin monotherapy increased the risk for stroke by 20%, combined CVD endpoint by 25%, angina by 16%, and doubled the risk for HF relative to chlorthalidone monotherapy. These data were reviewed and it was deemed unethical to continue the doxazosin arm so it was stopped while the other 3 arms (chlorthalidone, lisinopril, amlodipine) in the study were continued.

  - Interim analyses are best reviewed by an independent data and safety monitoring committee to minimize bias from trial sponsors and investigators.

Through their review, this committee not only helps ensure patient safety, but also data integrity and has the authority to continue or stop a trial early regardless of sponsor or investigator opinion.[20]

- **Types of Interim Analyses (alpha spending functions)**

    - **Haybittle-Peto** is a conservative early stopping rule with almost no impact on final analysis significance level.[20]

    - **Pocock fixed nominal levels** has a liberal stopping rule so there is a significant impact on the final analysis significance level.[20]

    - **O'Brien Fleming** is a trial stopping boundary technique that is appropriate for use with multiple interim analyses. At the beginning of the trial, it is more difficult to stop the trial with this analysis. But as the trial proceeds forward in time (i.e., as evidence accumulates), true statistically significant differences are more easily detected such that the trial may be stopped more easily. It is a conservative early stopping rule (especially for the 1st interim analysis) with almost no impact on final analysis significance level.[20]

        - **Lan and DeMets** is a version of O'Brien Fleming that allows flexibility in the number and timing of interim analyses used.

▪ Multiple Analyses

When making either multiple comparisons between 2 groups or a single comparison between multiple groups, type 1 error risk increases.

For example, when rolling dice, think of rolling ones on both dice (snake eyes) as being a type 1 error. For each roll of the dice there is a 1 in 36 chance (2.78%) of rolling snake eyes. For each statistical analysis, we generally accept a 1 in 20 chance (5%) of a type 1 error. Although the chance for snake eyes is the same for each roll and the chance for type 1 error is the same for each analysis, increasing the number of rolls and analyses increases the opportunity for snake eyes and type 1 errors, respectively.

Said another way, the more times one rolls the dice, the more opportunity one has to roll snake eyes. It's the same with statistical testing. The more times one performs a statistical test on a particular data set, whether it be multiple comparisons of 2 groups, a single comparison of multiple groups, or multiple comparisons of multiple groups, the more likely one is to commit a type 1 error.

Example 1: A **single comparison of multiple groups** for which the authors and/or statisticians did not make type 1 error risk corrections.

- A trial evaluated the difference in all-cause mortality between pravastatin, simvastatin, atorvastatin, and rosuvastatin. First, we need to determine the number of comparisons that were made. In this example, **one endpoint (difference in all-cause mortality)** was evaluated for **four lipid lowering medication groups (pravastatin, simvastatin, atorvastatin, and rosuvastatin)**. For the following equations, C represents the calculated number of comparisons, X represents the number of groups being studied, and NEE represents the number of endpoints being evaluated.

  C = {[X(X-1)]/2} (NEE)

  X = 4 groups (lipid lowering medications); NEE = 1 (all-cause mortality), so...

  C = {[4(4-1)]/2} (1)= (12/2)(1) = (6)(1) = 6 comparisons were made.

- We now need to determine the type 1 error risk if the investigators did not control for type 1 error risk.

  Corrected $\alpha = 1-(1-\alpha)^{c} = 1-(1-0.05)^{6} = 0.26$

- Therefore, if the original p-value threshold of 0.05 were used, there would be a 26% chance of inappropriately rejecting the null hypothesis (type 1 error) for at least one of the 6 comparisons.[4]

Example 2: **Multiple comparisons of 2 groups** for which the authors and/or statisticians did not make type 1 error risk corrections.

- A trial evaluated chlorthalidone vs hydrochlorothiazide (HCTZ) for the primary endpoint of all-cause mortality. In addition to this, there were other evaluated endpoints: any cardiovascular (CV) endpoint, stroke, MI, and hospitalization. First, we need to determine the number of comparisons that were made. In this example, **five endpoints (all-cause mortality, any CV endpoint, stroke, MI, hospitalization)** were evaluated for **two blood pressure medication groups (chlorthalidone and HCTZ)**. For the following equations, C represents the calculated number of comparisons, X represents the number of groups being studied, and NEE represents the number of endpoints being evaluated.

  C = {[X(X-1)]/2} (NEE)

-

  X = 2 groups (chlorthalidone and HCTZ); NEE = 5 (all-cause mortality, any CV endpoint, stroke, MI, hospitalization)

  C = {[2(2-1)]/2} (5) = (2/2)(5) = (1)(5) = 5 comparisons being made.

- We now need to determine the type 1 error risk if the investigators did not control for type 1 error risk.

  Corrected $\alpha = 1-(1-\alpha)^{c} = 1-(1-0.05)^{5} = 0.23$

- Therefore, if the original p-value threshold of 0.05 were used, there would be a 23% chance of inappropriately rejecting the null hypothesis (type 1 error) for at least one of the 5 comparisons.[4]

Example 3: **<u>Multiple comparisons of multiple groups</u>** for which the authors and/or statisticians did not make type 1 error risk corrections.

- A trial evaluated metformin, glipizide, and exenatide for the primary endpoint of A1c. In addition to this, there were other evaluated endpoints: fasting blood glucose (FBG), SCr, total cholesterol (TC), low density lipoprotein cholesterol (LDL), high density lipoprotein cholesterol (HDL), and triglycerides (TG). First, we need to determine the number of comparisons that were made. In this example, **seven endpoints (A1c, FBG, SCr, TC, LDL, HDL, TG)** were evaluated for **three diabetes medication groups (metformin, glipizide, and exenatide)**. For the following equations, C represents the calculated number of comparisons, X represents the number of groups being studied, and NEE represents the number of endpoints being evaluated.

- C = {[X(X-1)]/2} (NEE)

  X = 3 groups (three diabetes medications); NEE = 7 (A1c, FBG, SCr, TC, LDL, HDL, TG)

  C = {[3(3-1)]/2} (7) = (6/2)(7) = (3)(7) = 21 comparisons being made.

- We now need to determine the type 1 error risk if the investigators did not control for type 1 error risk.

  Corrected $\alpha = 1-(1-\alpha)^{c} = 1-(1-0.05)^{21} = 0.66$

- Therefore, if the original p-value threshold of 0.05 were used, there would be a 66% chance of inappropriately rejecting the null hypothesis (type 1 error) for at least one of the 21 comparisons.[4]

Use the above calculations to estimate type 1 error risk when investigators fail to control for multiple comparisons.

Investigators should make an effort to keep the type 1 error risk ≤ 5% (i.e., ≤0.05). The best way of doing so for multiple comparisons is by avoiding unnecessary comparisons or analyses, using the appropriate statistical test(s) for multiple comparisons, and using an alpha spending function for interim

analyses. (see pages 170-171 for alpha spending function and interim analyses) However, if investigators fail to do so, there is a crude method for adjusting the preset α level based upon the number of comparisons being made: the **Bonferroni correction**. This simply divides the preset α level by the number of comparisons being made.[4] This estimates the α level that is required to reach statistical significance.[4]

Bonferroni is very conservative as the number of comparisons increases.[11] **Use the following method/calculation when investigators fail to control for multiple comparisons.**

Bonferroni correction for example 1:

$$\alpha_{adj} = \frac{\alpha_p}{\text{\# of comparisons}} \qquad \alpha_{adj} = \frac{0.05}{6} = 0.008$$

Based upon this Bonferroni correction, requiring the p-value to be ≤ 0.008 would ensure that type 1 error risk would not exceed 5%.[4]

Bonferroni correction for example 2:

$$\alpha_{adj} = \frac{\alpha_p}{\text{\# of comparisons}} \qquad \alpha_{adj} = \frac{0.05}{5} = 0.01$$

Based upon this Bonferroni correction, requiring the p-value to be ≤ 0.01 would ensure that type 1 error risk would not exceed 5%.[4]

Bonferroni correction for example 3:

$$\alpha_{adj} = \frac{\alpha_p}{\text{\# of comparisons}} \qquad \alpha_{adj} = \frac{0.05}{21} = 0.0024$$

Based upon this Bonferroni correction, requiring the p-value to be ≤ 0.0024 would ensure that type 1 error risk would not exceed 5%.[4]

See pages 76-79 for more Bonferroni correction examples.

There are a number of methods that are less conservative than Bonferroni for controlling type 1 error risk for multiple analyses.

- ANOVA and its multiple comparison methods were already discussed under the parametric data section of this book.

- Other methods that are more powerful (less conservative) than Bonferroni are Sidak, Dunn-Sidak, Bonferroni Holm, Holm step-down (aka Holm step-down Bonferroni), Benjamini-Hochberg, Hommel, Fisher combination method, Westfall and Young permutation, and Hochberg step-up method (aka Hochberg step-up

Bonferroni or Hochberg multiplicity method). The more powerful (i.e., less conservative) the method, the more likely true statistically significant differences will be detected.

There are also times when unnecessary multiple analyses are performed. For example, some researchers perform post hoc tests in the absence of a statistically significant χ^2, Kruskal-Wallis, Friedman, or ANOVA tests. Another example is how some researchers perform statistical tests to detect differences in baseline characteristics between groups in hopes of detecting potential confounders. However, this strategy is flawed for the following reasons:[36]

- Differences between baseline characteristics do not indicate the amount confounding present in a data set. Of the conditions which help determine if a particular factor is a confounder, difference in baseline characteristics is just one.[36]

- "Assessment of confounding requires understanding of the degree of association between the factor, exposure, and outcome, but statistical significance testing depends upon the sample size and degree of association being evaluated."[36]

- When performing statistical significance testing for baseline characteristics, the null hypothesis is that no difference exists between the groups. Therefore, if a statistically significant difference is detected, the null hypothesis must be rejected which would be interpreted as randomization failure.[36]

"It makes much more sense to examine the relationship between the factor, exposure, and event. Methods to accomplish this include descriptive techniques, such as graphs and tables, as well as correlation and regression models."[36]

▪ Subgroup Analysis (SA)

- There are two general types of subgroup analyses: (1) *post hoc* (formulated after the fact) or (2) *a priori* (conceived beforehand).[27]

- All ***post hoc*** **SAs** "should be considered hypothesis-generating as they typically have insufficient power to detect differences, are subject to biases that are not accounted for in the initial randomization, and present more opportunities for spurious results as a consequence of multiple comparisons. Significant differences that are suggested by post hoc subgroups should be further confirmed in subsequent" prospective, controlled trials.[27]

- ***a priori*** **SAs** "can be analyzed in the same manner as any H_o. Whether the subgroups make sense clinically is not guaranteed and must be considered when drawing conclusions. However, if the divisions suggested provide useful information, then their statistical analysis would proceed along" as usual.

"Deliberations about power and multiple comparisons take on a heightened importance when deciding whether suggested differences should be trusted."[27] Generally, trials are not originally powered to detect statistically significant differences for subgroups. When dividing patients into subgroups, one may increase the ability to detect a statistically significant difference in one group while decreasing the ability to do so in another group. One must consider the number of patients being evaluated in each subgroup, the incidence of the outcome being evaluated for each subgroup, and any confounding variables to better utilize these data. When used appropriately, *a priori* SAs "can provide a more refined understanding about the effects of a drug therapy." There may be a case where a drug provides benefit for a sample of patients and additional benefit for a subgroup of those same patients.[27] In most cases, significant differences detected by SAs should be further confirmed in subsequent prospective, controlled trials.[27] For example, in the VHeFT trial, there were positive results for all patients treated with isosorbide/hydralazine. However, the results were more impressive in the black subgroup than in the non-black subgroup. This benefit led to studying the addition of isosorbide/hydralazine to standard of care therapy in solely self-proclaimed African-American patients in the AHeFT trial.

Example of an *a priori* SA: In the ValHeFT trial, some subgroup analyses were presented as follows. Valsartan appeared to be beneficial in decreasing morbidity/mortality in:

- **Patients <65 yrs old (n = 2660)**, but not patients ≥ 65 yrs old (n = 2350)
- **Males (n = 4007)**, but not females (n = 1003)
- Patients **without Ischemic heart disease (n = 2145)**, but not patients with Ischemic heart disease (n = 2865)
- Patients **without Diabetes (n = 3734)**, but not patients with Diabetes (n = 1276)
- **NYHA class 3** and 4 (n = 1910), but not patients with Class 2 HF (n = 3095)
- **EF ≤27% (n = 2385),** but not EF ≥27% (n = 2623)
- Left Ventricular Internal Diastolic Diameter **(LVIDD) ≥3.57 cm/m^2**(n = 2505), but not patients with LVIDD < 3.57 cm/m^2 (n = 2505)
    - Look at the **male vs female** subgroups. Simply based upon the **number of subjects** in each subgroup alone, there is deference in the ability to detect a statistically significant difference. The number of patients in each subgroup is unequal. There were 4007 males, but only 1003

females. So one would be more likely to detect a difference (whether good or bad) in the group of males if a difference truly exists.

- In addition, one would **expect males to have more adverse cardiac outcomes anyway**. Yet another reason one would more likely detect a difference (whether good or bad) in the male group if a difference truly exists.

- When evaluating **EF**, these patients appear to be fairly evenly divided... with even more patients in the EF≥ 27% group. So there should be a fairly equal ability of detecting a difference in these groups right? Maybe even more of an ability in the EF≥ 27% group right?

    - Well, maybe not. Sometimes one group may be more likely to experience an outcome than another group. In this example, one would expect patients with a lower EF (i.e., sicker patients) to actually experience more endpoints than the healthier patients. In other words, **expected incidence would be higher in the group with sicker patients (patients with EF<27%).** Remember that as incidence of a particular outcome increases, the sample size required decreases. (i.e., do not need as many patients in the sample to detect a true difference) So, in the case of patients with lower EFs, since these patients are sicker, one would expect more endpoints to be experienced (i.e., a higher incidence and this may be the reason a statistically significant difference was found in the patients with an EF<27%.

    - This does not mean that no difference exists between valsartan and placebo for healthier patients. (patients with EF≥ 27%) **Maybe since incidence is lower in the healthier patients, more patients are needed to show a difference between Valsartan and placebo.**

    - **Same goes for NYHA class and LV internal diastolic diameter.** More patients may be required to show a true difference between Valsartan and placebo for the healthier patients. Also, note that **only 1.9%** of patients in this study **had NYHA class 4**. So there are insufficient data to make any claims of Valsartan's efficacy with regard to Class 4 HF patients.

- How about **Diabetes**? One would expect patients with diabetes to experience more CV endpoints, and therefore demonstrate any true statistically significant improvements more easily than non-diabetic patients.

    - So why did the investigators detect a difference in the subgroup without diabetes? Furthermore, why was no difference detected in the subgroup with diabetes? → At the start of this trial, **only 25% of the subjects had Diabetes**, which greatly decreases power to detect a difference when one truly exists. Look at the raw numbers. Only 1276 patients with diabetes were analyzed. So lack of power could be responsible for the non-statistically significant improvement.

- Now when evaluating the **coexisting ischemic heart disease** subgroup, the numbers of patients as well as expected incidence for an outcome would favor finding a difference in the group with ischemic heart disease.
  - However, this trial actually demonstrated a difference only in the patients without ischemic heart disease. But endpoints in patients with ischemic heart disease are pretty susceptible to confounding. In other words, **these patients die or are hospitalized for lots of reasons other than HF, which is what these investigators tried to avoid as was mentioned in the exclusion criteria** section of this trial.
  - It seems indicative that the ARB may not be beneficial for patients with pre-existing Ischemic Heart disease. However, this remains to be seen with future trials.

- **p for interaction (aka p-value for interaction)** simply detects heterogeneity among subgroups. A significant p for interaction generally ranges from 0.05 to 0.1 depending on the analysis. In other words if a subgroup analysis finds a p for interaction < 0.05 (or <0.1 for some studies) for patients with versus without diabetes, then there is a significant difference in treatment effect based upon diabetes diagnosis. This difference may be worth investigating in future analyses. Just as with other types of subgroups analyses, p for interaction solely detects hypothesis generating differences.

- ## Survival Analysis

- **Survival analysis** "studies the time between entry into a study and some event."[8] The endpoint of survival analysis does not have to be death. It could be treatment response, hospitalization, development of a disease, worsening or improvement of a disease or any of a number of other nominal endpoints. Survival analyses can be performed with Cohort and RCTs.
  - **Independent variable**: the intervention for a RCT... or the exposure for a cohort study.
  - **Dependent variable**: time to the event.
    - **The endpoint (or event) does <u>not</u> have to be something negative like death, hospitalization, or development of a disease. It could be something positive like treatment response.**
  - Patients are followed until they either experience a predefined event or follow-up is terminated without the occurrence of an endpoint.
    - Survival analysis "uses survival times (or **censored survival times**) to estimate the proportion of people who would 'survive' a **given length of time** under the same circumstances."[8,11]
    - **Censored survival times**: in a given study not everyone will reach the endpoint.[8,11]
      - For example, if the outcome is death, there are some patients who will not die before the end of the trial.[31,32] Others may be lost to follow-up such that it is unknown if they are alive or dead at the end of the trial.[31,32] Still others may have died from a reason unrelated to the study, as may be the case in a motor vehicle accident fatality. This group may be either included in the analysis or censored.[8,11,32] Censored survival times take all of these circumstances into consideration.[11]
      - Also, as one moves forward in time, sample size (n) decreases (i.e., the denominator continues to shrink).[11] So log-rank analysis is used to account for loss of sample patients.
        - Example: If 5 patients die every month in a sample of 100 patients, the probability of surviving for 3 months =100 – (3x5)/100 = 85/100 = 0.85

      or...
        - 95/100 x 90/95 x 85/90 = 0.85

- Also when patients are lost to follow-up, data that were collected until the time the patient was lost to follow-up can be utilized.

- Depending upon how the survival curve is graphically represented, it may represent either 1) the probability of **NOT** having an event, or 2) the probability of having an event within a certain time period. (see graphs below)

  - **Median Survival time**: the time corresponding to an estimated probability of survival of 0.5.... or 50%.

- **Hazard**: the probability of an event during a specified time interval. Hazards may or may not (as in Kaplan-Meier method) change over time.

- The life table method calculates the cumulative probability of surviving over a period of time.

  - There are **two ways to calculate a life table**.

    - **Actuarial Method is rarely seen in clinical trial**

      - With the actuarial method, the probability of an event is assessed at a predefined interval.

      - Calculates survival function at fixed time interval (e.g., every month or year)

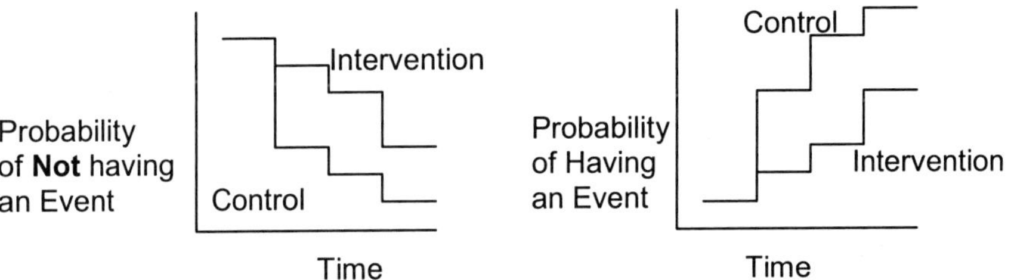

    - **Kaplan-Meier Method is <u>commonly seen in clinical trials</u> and <u>uses time interval to event</u> rather than set lengths of time** like months, years, etc., as was seen in the actuarial method.

      - With Kaplan Meier, the probability of an event changes only when an endpoint event occurs. (i.e., not at predefined intervals as would be the case with the actuarial method) Therefore, the Kaplan-Meier survival curve is horizontal between events. If there are a lot of events, there may be more of a "curve" rather than flat points or horizontal lines, ergo the terminology survival "curve".

- As the numbers of subjects decline with event occurrences and censored observations, precision decreases. (i.e., greater data variability/spread).

- **Kaplan-Meier ALWAYS uses log-rank tests to test for statistically significant differences between groups.**[11] (see below) **Log rank tests can only test for one variable at a time.**[8]

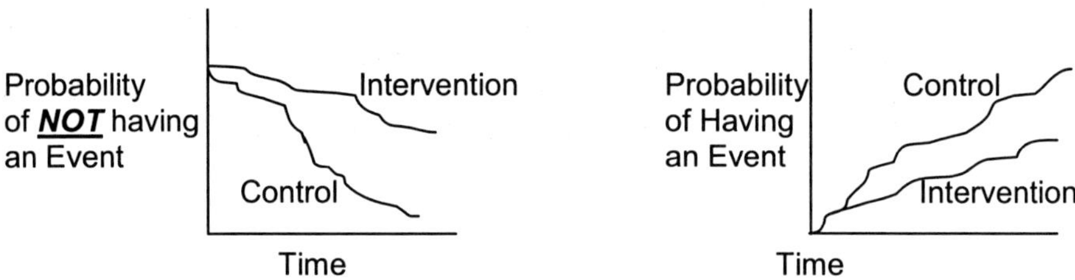

- **Statistical Tests for Survival Analysis**. Many statistical tests have been developed to compare survival curves. These compare the entire curve under H_o and do not compare any specific point in time along the curves. For superiority trials, H_o represents that no difference between the curves exists.

  - **Log-rank tests are ALWAYS used for Kaplan-Meier** to test "for statistically significant differences between groups."[8] Log rank tests are used when the ratio of hazards for 2 curves does not change over time, as would be the case for exponential survival curves that have constant hazards. (i.e., **log rank tests can only test the differences of one variable at a time, not several**)

  - **Wilcoxon-type tests** (e.g., **Gehan's generalized Wilcoxon** analysis of times to an event is very similar to Wilcoxon rank sum and Mann-Whitney U). These are **used when the ratio of hazards is not constant**. Gehan-Wilcoxon gives more weight to deaths at early time points whereas log-rank tests give equal weight to all time points. Gehan-Wilcoxon can be misleading when a large percentage of patients are censored at early time points.

  - **Cox Proportion Hazards** model (aka proportional hazards regression analysis or Cox regression model)

    - As with the others, Cox **tests if the difference between life table curves is statistically significant, but it can investigate several variables** at a time.[8] (can help account for confounders)

- Cox Proportion Regression Analysis can utilize **time-varying covariates** whose values are able to change over time such that the "model can correctly account for HRs that vary over the course of a study."[35] For example, for some surgeries, the mortality rate is higher 1 month after surgery relative to 1 year post-op. Cox can account for this.

- **Hazard Ratio (HR)** is used with Cox Proportion Hazards Regression analysis. (ANBP2, page 585)

    - HR is used when a study is evaluating the length of time required for an outcome of interest to occur.[35] HR is often used similarly to RR, and is a reasonable estimate of RR as long as adequate data are collected and outcome incidence is <15%.[35] However, whereas RR only represents the probability of having an event between the beginning and end of a study, HR represents the probability of having an event during a certain time interval between the beginning and end of the study.[27]

- **Systematic Reviews** are a collection of high quality trials that help answer questions not previously answered by individual trials. These typically only include high-quality RCTs. Meta-analysis helps synthesize and quantitatively evaluate information from systematic reviews.

- **Meta-Analyses (MA)** quantitatively synthesize data from multiple studies to help answer questions not previously answered by individual studies.[44] High quality MAs only include well conducted RCTs. However, some MAs include lower quality studies like cohort or case-control studies which decrease their validity as it pertains to causality.

- If performed correctly, MA is "a thorough review of the published (and sometimes unpublished) literature regarding a particular question and includes a statistical analysis of the pooled results."[29] In other words, investigators take lots of parts (multiple studies), then put these together to help find information leading to final resolution of some particular question.[9,11] A MA "looks at the results within each study and calculates a weighted average."[31]

  - "The **Cochrane Collaboration** is an international group of health care professionals and epidemiologists that, on a continual basis, prepares, maintains, and disseminates meta-analyses. More information about this group can be found at *http://www.cochrane.org*."[29]

  - **MAs are used to**:

    - answer questions not answered with prior research, especially when prior studies lacked power to detect differences between groups.[29]

    - decrease the risk of a type 2 error by increasing power via increased sample size through combining multiple studies.[29]

    - generate hypotheses to be evaluated in studies.[29]

    - calculate estimated <u>sample</u> size required to detect meaningful difference(s).[29]

    - calculate <u>effect</u> size: help determine **the degree** of benefit/harm from the intervention. (i.e., not just is there benefit/harm)[9] The denominator is usually SD. The numerator may be many things: r or mmHg, etc.

  - **Statistical analyses used in MAs**

    - "Heterogeneity refers to the variability or differences between studies...."[26]

- Types of heterogeneity include:
  - Methodological heterogeneity: differences in study design and execution: parallel vs cross-over, ITT vs As-Treated analysis, etc.[26,31]
  - Clinical heterogeneity: differences in interventions, outcomes, and participant demographics and comorbidities.[26,31]
  - Statistical heterogeneity: more variability in reported effects than would be expected by chance alone.[26,31]
    - Initially **a test of heterogeneity**, like a **Breslow Day** Test, is performed to detect if the results of various studies (i.e., data analysis results and conclusions) are heterogeneous. This type of test assesses if the observed variability in the individual study results is "greater than that expected to occur by chance".[26]
    - **Tests of heterogeneity** include:
      - **Breslow Day Test**: For this test, if the Breslow Day p-value is below the pre-specified α level, heterogeneity is present. The α level is usually either <0.05 or <0.10. An α of 0.10 is typically reserved for MAs including only a few studies, whereas an α of 0.05 is typically used for MAs including a lot of studies. This is because less data decrease power for detecting heterogeneity and more data increase power for detecting heterogeneity.[31]
      - **Chi-square (χ^2) statistic vs degrees of freedom (df or dof):** Some MAs provide a comparison of a chi-square (χ^2) statistic vs its degrees of freedom. If the χ^2 statistic is greater than its degrees of freedom, then heterogeneity is present.[31]
      - $\boldsymbol{I^2}$: Some MAs use I^2 to test for heterogeneity. I^2 ranges from 0% to 100% heterogeneity. The higher the I^2 value, the more heterogeneity present. An I^2 of 0% would mean an absolute absence of heterogeneity.[27]

        "Thresholds for the interpretation of I^2 can be misleading, since the importance of inconsistency depends on several factors. A rough guide to interpretation is as follows:

        - 0% to 40%: might not be important;
        - 30% to 60%: may represent moderate heterogeneity*;
        - 50% to 90%: may represent substantial heterogeneity*;

- 75% to 100%: considerable heterogeneity*.

*The importance of the observed value of I^2 depends on (i) magnitude and direction of effects and (ii) strength of evidence for heterogeneity (e.g. p-value from the chi-squared test, or a confidence interval for I^2)." [43]

- **Cochran Q**: Small MAs may use Cochran Q. If the Q statistic p-value is below the pre-specified α level, heterogeneity is present. The α level is usually either <0.05 or <0.10. An α of 0.1 is typically reserved for MAs including fewer studies, whereas an α of 0.05 is typically used for MAs including more studies. This is because less data decrease power for detecting heterogeneity and more data increase power for detecting heterogeneity.[31]

- **Forest Plot**: Some MAs provide a Forest Plot to detect heterogeneity visually.[31] (see the following Forest Plot example below)

- **If heterogeneity is <u>not</u> detected**, a fixed effects model like **Mantel Haenszel** should be used since there is no need to control for variation between study results.

- **If heterogeneity is detected**, then a random-effects model like **DerSimonian and Laird** should be used to control for variation between study results. Random-effects models like the method developed by DerSimonian and Laird allow for the possibility that the true treatment effect may vary from study to study.

  - For example, if the preset acceptable alpha is 0.1 and the Breslow Day Test, or some other test for heterogeneity, produces a p>0.1, a fixed-effects model like Mantel-Haenszel should be used as the statistical test to determine statistical significance of the MA results since controlling for variability in the individual study results is not required. If the Breslow Day Test, or some other test for heterogeneity, produces a p≤0.1, then a random-effects model like DerSimonian and Laird is the required statistical test to determine statistical significance of the MA results since one has to control for variability in the individual study results.

- **Some MA authors perform both fixed- and random-effects models.** This is not an issue as long as the authors report the most appropriate result(s); generally the model with the most conservative outcome estimate(s).[31]

- **What if the MA did not perform heterogeneity testing?**
  - You will see this sometimes. Most of the time the authors will use a random-effects model to account for any possible variability between the individual study results. However random-effects models are more conservative than fixed-effects models. (i.e., random-effects models are less likely to detect statistically significant differences when present) So if the MA authors used a random-effects model without testing for heterogeneity, one needs to question if the authors are trying to sway the MA results toward their opinion(s).
  - For example, let's say that I am of the opinion that studied β-blockers are just as beneficial for systolic dysfunction heart failure (HF) in geriatric patients as they are in younger patients. Since there is not an available RCT that is powerful enough to meaningfully assess differences in this age group with regard to HF outcomes, I will conduct a MA.
    - Remember that I want to show no difference between the groups so I can produce data that support my position. I am less likely to find a difference between the age groups with regard to HF outcomes if I inappropriately use a random-effects model.
    - My results would have been more trustworthy and clinically meaningful if I had first performed a heterogeneity test like Breslow Day and then used its results to determine the appropriate statistical method (i.e., fixed- vs random-effects model) to evaluate the MA.

- **Forest Plot**: Results of MAs may be presented in a **Forest plot**

Outcome: Relative Risk for death	Weight (%)	RR (95%CI)
Study 1	7.3	0.83 (0.56 - 1.11)
Study 2	4.7	0.63 (0.33 - 0.93)
Study 3	9.5	0.82 (0.61 - 1.05)
Study 4	11.4	0.80 (0.62 - 0.95)
Study 5	1.2	0.69 (0.3 - 1.12)
Study 6	32.9	0.76 (0.63 - 0.87)
Study 7	14.4	0.74 (0.60 - 0.92)
Study 8	5.7	0.87 (0.57 - 1.16)
Study 9	12.9	0.71 (0.55 - 0.87)
Total (95%CI)	100	0.76 (0.67 - 0.81)

Favors Experimental Group — 1.0 — Favors Control Group

Note that **larger, more heavily weighted studies have larger point estimate boxes and narrower confidence intervals (CI)**.

- **Evaluation of MAs:**

  - Were included studies appropriate? Did it make sense to include the studies that were included? It would be senseless to include studies with so many differences that the results would be meaningless.[31] (e.g., including case control and RCTs in the MA) Ideally, the MA would include similar patients, settings, interventions, outcomes, statistical methods, etc.

  - Was it appropriate for the authors to pool results? If authors expected outcomes to differ between studies based upon groups evaluated, setting of study, length of study, etc., then pooling results may be inappropriate.[31]

  - Did the author(s) point out planned vs. "post hoc" analyses?[31]

  - **Sensitivity analysis**: are the findings of the MA substantially influenced by the way the analysis was conducted?

    - Are the results driven by the inclusion of one or two larger studies? How do the results change if one removes the larger study (or studies) from the analysis? If the results do not change then one can say that the results of the MA are not dependent upon the larger study, but are supported by the rest of the studies included in the MA.[9,31]

        - Was the influential study an outlier?[31]
        - Was there some doubt about the study's eligibility criteria?[31]
        - Was the study of poor quality relative to the others included in the MA?[31]

    - Were the results dependent upon fixed vs random effects model? To answer this question, it would be important for the authors to analyze the MA data both ways.[31]
    - How did different imputation methods (LOCF vs estimated vs worst case scenario) for missing data influence the MA result(s)?[31]

- **Weaknesses of MAs:**
    - Results highly reliant upon the quality of included studies.[9]
    - Subject to selection bias.
        - Depending upon their skills, knowledge, and contacts, different researchers may find a different list of studies to include and evaluate.
        - Were non-English studies included?
    - Subject to publication bias.
        - Studies are not typically of the same quality.[31]
        - Publication bias: studies with significant results, especially positive results, are more likely to be published. This would obviously bias the MA. When able, unpublished studies should be included in MAs.[9,11,31]

Some MAs use a **Funnel Plot to identify publication bias**, but unfortunately, as explained below, funnel plots are not reliable predictors of publication bias.[31]

One would expect the funnel plot to be symmetrical if little to no publication bias is present. Unfortunately, symmetrical funnel plots do not assure absence of publication bias.[31]

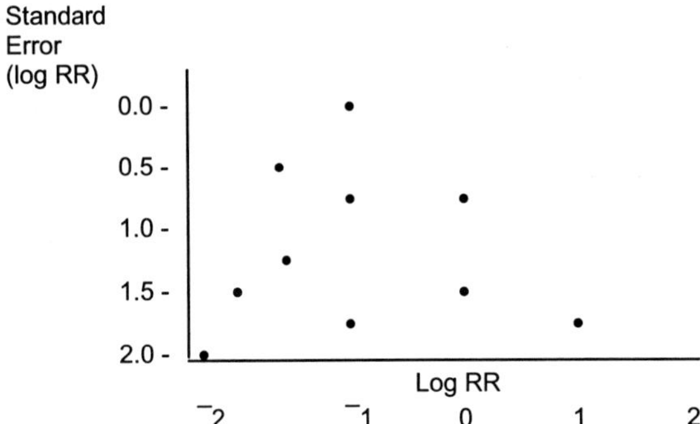

The "hollow plot" below is symmetrical, but indicates publication bias. There are studies indicating a positive or negative difference, but there are no studies indicating "no difference". Remember that studies are more likely to be published if a significant difference is found; especially if the difference is a positive difference.

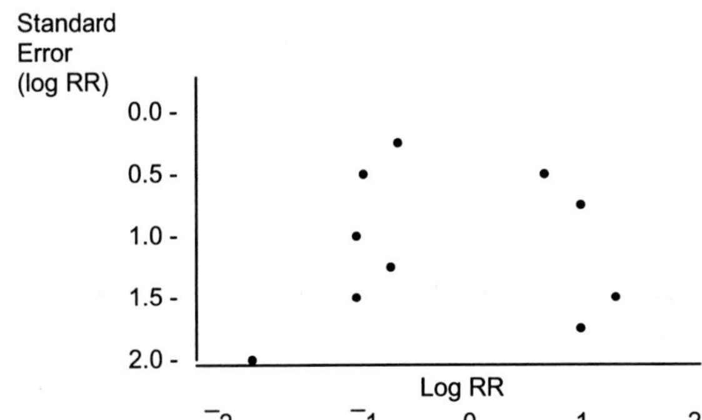

Neither does an asymmetrical plot assure presence of publication bias.[31]

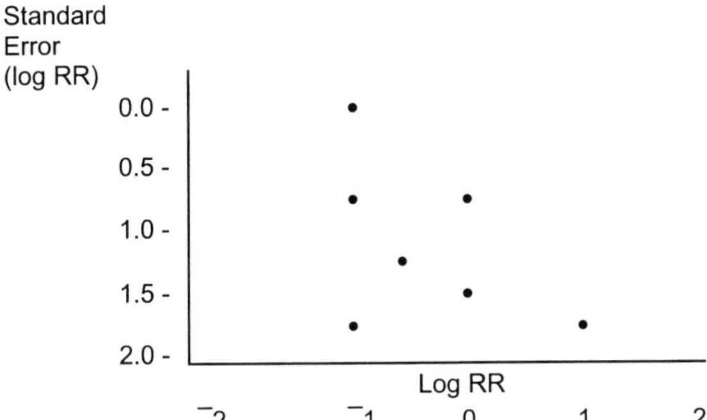

An asymmetrical plot may indicate:

- publication bias.[31]
- the MA included poorer quality studies.[31] This is especially problematic when a study is unblinded and therefore more likely to have an exaggerated effect size. This is an example of how methodological heterogeneity (lack of blinding) can adversely affect MA results.[31]
- the MA included a study conducted in a high risk group, which may increase effect size.[31]
- "clinical heterogeneity between studies… e.g., different control event rates."[31]

Statistical tests like **Egger's Linear Regression Test** and **Begg's Rank Correlation Test** are sometimes used to detect funnel plot asymmetry, but these are low power tests.[31]

Additionally, there are some weak methods used to correct for publication bias. These include "Modeling", the "Fail safe N", and the "Trim and fill method".[31]

Study Questions:(many provided by Melanie Pound, PharmD, BCPS)

94. A subgroup analysis was performed on a trial's data set (n=5000 total patients). Prior to the initiation of this trial, the investigators decided upon which groups would be included in this analysis. This analysis indicated a statistically significant survival benefit only in female patients (n=4150). What may have been the reason for these discrepancies?
    - a. Differences in sample size may have decreased power to detect a difference in the male subgroup.
    - b. Differences in outcome incidences may have increased risk for a Type 2 error in the female subgroup.
    - c. Differences in confounders may have increased risk for a Type 2 error in the female subgroup.
    - d. A difference in survival benefit among males relative to females is likely correct and therefore hypothesis proving for this analysis.

(for the next 2 questions)
Your clinic team would like to determine if a new BP medication may be beneficial for your patients.

95. Which of the following should be your approach?
    - a. Review current data concerning BP lowering in a patient population similar to your clinic's patient population.
    - b. Review current data concerning cardiovascular (CV) endpoint differences in a patient population similar to your clinic's patient population.
    - c. Review current data concerning BP lowering, CV endpoint differences, and adverse effects (AE) in a patient population similar to your clinic's patient population.
    - d. Review current data concerning BP lowering and AE in a patient population similar to your clinic's patient population.

96. With one of the trials, the authors state that 2 interim analyses were performed to ensure patient safety. How might this affect the results of the trial?
    - a. Without proper controls (e.g. O'Brien Fleming), this would increase risk for a Type 1 error.
    - b. This would increase risk for Type 1 error.
    - c. Without proper controls (e.g. O'Brien Fleming), this would increase beta.
    - d. Without proper controls (e.g. O'Brien Fleming), this would decrease power.
    - e. This would not affect the trial results.

97. An investigator wishes to study a new drug, Camelapril, for the treatment of hypertension in patients with diabetes. This study evaluates the effects of BP lowering among the patients comparing their mean BP at baseline and at the end of the study. Their secondary endpoint is the side effects of the medications. Which of the following is the BEST way to analyze the data?
   a. Both the primary and secondary endpoints should be analyzed via ITT.
   b. Both the primary and secondary endpoints should be analyzed via per-protocol.
   c. Both the primary and secondary endpoints should be analyzed via as-treated.
   d. The primary endpoint should be analyzed via ITT, while the secondary endpoint should be analyzed via per-protocol.
   e. The primary endpoint should be analyzed via per-protocol, while the secondary endpoint should be analyzed via ITT.

98. A recent trial examined the use of aprotinin, aminocaproic acid and control during CABG surgery. The study investigators wish to perform a post-trial analysis evaluating low risk patients and their risk of mortality. Which of the following is(are) correct regarding this analysis?
   a. The results from this type of analysis may be considered data-dredging if it were not pre-specified.
   b. This will increase risk for type 1 error.
   c. This will increase risk for type 2 error.
   d. This will increase risk for delta error.
   e. Only "a" and "b" are correct answers

(for the next 2 questions)
A clinical trial is planned to evaluate the efficacy of a new medication (drug Z) compared to placebo in preventing complications of diabetes mellitus. Patients that are diagnosed with either nephropathy, neuropathy or retinopathy will be considered to have met the primary study endpoint. A Data Safety Monitoring Board will perform a planned interim analysis when approximately one-half of the subjects are enrolled in the clinical trial.

99. Which of the following accurately describes the appropriateness of an interim analysis for this study?
   a. An interim analysis avoids the risk of a "random high" in the data and therefore should avoid over-exaggerating differences
   b. The beta value used to determine study power should be divided by 2, because 2 analyses of the data (interim and final) will be performed.
   c. Rules for stopping the trial before all subjects are enrolled should be established at the start of the trial
   d. Use of such analysis is unethical, since the trial should continue regardless of interim results
   e. Both "b" and "c" are correct answers

100. Which of the following describes the type of endpoint(s) used in this study?

a. Surrogate endpoint
b. Composite endpoint
c. Raw endpoint
d. Retrospective endpoint
e. Both "a" and "c" are correct answers

Use the following table to answer the next 2 questions

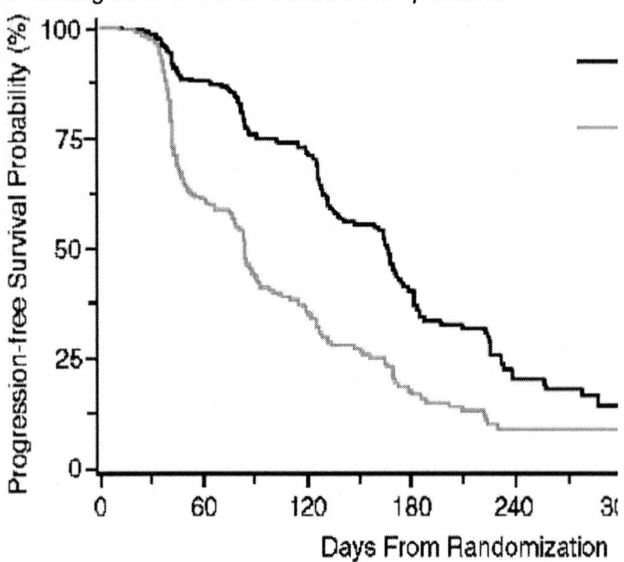

101. This is an example of which of the following?

a. Actuarial method life table
b. Kaplan Meier curve
c. Survival analysis
d. Forrest plot
e. Both "b" and "c" are correct answers

102. Which of the following is (are) true regarding the above graph?

a. This is a depiction of the probability of not having an "event" or "endpoint".
b. This type of analysis may test several variables at the same time.
c. A Cox proportional hazards ratio needs to be used to determine statistically significant differences between the groups.
d. This method is not able to utilize "censoring" for non-trial related data.
e. Log rank tests are <u>not</u> needed in this case.

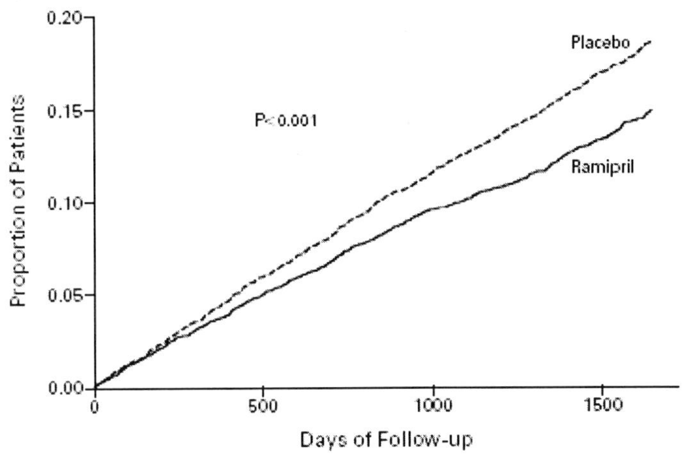

103. Which of the following is true regarding the above graph?
   a. This type is a depiction of a Kaplan-Meier curve.
   b. This is a depiction of the probability of having an "event" or "endpoint".
   c. A Cox proportional hazards ratio needs to be used to determine statistically significant differences b/n the groups.
   d. This method is not able to utilize "censoring" for non-trial related data.
   e. Both “a” and “b” are correct.

104. What test is always used to test for statistically significant differences between Kaplan-Meier curves?

105. Log rank tests can test for differences in ______ variable(s) at a time.

(for the next 9 questions)
An analysis is conducted evaluating the benefits of beta-blockers in elderly vs non-elderly patients and a history of systolic heart failure with regard to all-cause mortality and hospitalization due to heart failure. Some of the studies included in this analysis evaluate Toprol XL with doses up to 200mg daily and some evaluate Coreg with doses up to 50mg twice daily.

106. What type of analysis is this?
   a. RCT
   b. Case-series
   c. Meta-analysis
   d. Prospective Cohort
   e. Retrospective Cohort

107. How could the authors minimize publication bias?
   a. Include English and non-English language studies
   b. Include published and unpublished studies
   c. Include well known and lesser known studies
   d. Include studies meeting inclusion criteria, regardless of the studies' findings: positive, negative, or neutral.
   e. All of the above answers are correct

108. Which of the following would not help assess the need to perform either a fixed or random effects model?
   a. Breslow Day Test
   b. Mantel Haenszel
   c. chi-square vs degrees of freedom
   d. I^2
   e. Cochran Q

109. If an alpha cut-point of 0.1 is used for the heterogeneity test and p = 0.07 for heterogeneity, which of the following tests should be to help analyze the pooled data for this analysis?
   a. Breslow Day Test
   b. Mantel Haenszel
   c. DerSimonian and Laird
   d. Fixed effects test
   e. All of the above answers are correct

110. If an alpha cut-point of 0.05 is used for the heterogeneity test and p = 0.07 for heterogeneity, which of the following tests should be to help analyze the pooled data for this analysis?
   a. Breslow Day Test
   b. A fixed effects model like Mantel Haenszel
   c. DerSimonian and Laird
   d. Random effects model
   e. All of the above answers are correct

111. Which of the following regarding this analysis is TRUE?
   a. Increasing sample size increases both power and risk for a type 2 error
   b. Increasing power decreases the ability to detect meaningful differences
   c. Different researchers would include the same study
   d. It would be more difficult to analyze studies with different designs than studies with similar designs
   e. The meta-analysis is hypothesis proving

112. The researchers want to evaluate the risk that one or two studies is/are more influential than the others. What may help with this evaluation?
    a. Sensitivity analysis
    b. Publication bias analysis
    c. Heterogeneity analysis
    d. Funnel plot analysis
    e. All of the above are correct

113. After an exhaustive search by all of the authors, they note that all of the publications detect differences between elderly and non-elderly patients. Some of the publications support and some refute the benefit(s) of beta-blockers in elderly patients with a history of systolic dysfunction heart failure. What is the likely cause of this scenario?
    a. Selection bias
    b. Publication bias
    c. Homogeneity
    d. Funnel plot asymmetry
    e. All of the above are correct

114. If the authors had noted all of the publications detect either benefit or no difference at all in elderly vs non-elderly patients, of what might this have been an indication?
    a. Inclusion of poor quality studies
    b. Publication bias
    c. Inclusion of high-risk patient studies
    d. Variability in control group event rates
    e. All of the above are correct

Answers to Study Questions:

94. a - There were only 850 male vs 4150 female patients, so this may have decreased power to detect a difference in the male group. Since a difference was found in the female group, a type 2 error could not have occurred.

95. c - Surrogate endpoints are fine for some disease states, but are not as important as clinical outcomes for disease states like hypertension.

96. a

97. d - ITT should be used for the primary endpoint because it is the most “real world” scenario and gives the most conservative endpoint estimate. Per protocol should be used for side effects since it will give a clearer picture of what side effects actually occur with the studied medications. Since ITT and mITT analyze based upon initial assignment rather than what patients actually received, and regardless of medication adherence, these would not provide a true picture of medications’ side effect profiles. Since As-treated analyzes data regardless of medication adherence, it would not provide a true picture of medications’ side effect profiles.

98. e - There is no such thing as “delta error”. Post-hoc analyses that are not prespecified are considered data dredging. Non-prespecified post-hoc analyses increase the number of analyses performed on a data set without proper planned procedures in place, so these increase type 1 error risk.

99. c - Rules for stopping a trial early should be established before the trial begins. There very well may be a “random high” or over-exaggeration of differences before all data are collected, so an interim analysis will not protect against this. Some interim analyses divide the alpha value (not the beta value) by the number of analyses performed. Interim analyses are ethical. In fact, their purpose is to help ensure patient safety.

100. b - These are clinical endpoints, not surrogate endpoints. Since ≥ 2 (three in this case) outcomes (nephropathy, neuropathy, or retinopathy) serve as the primary study endpoint of “complications”, this is a composite endpoint. There is no such thing as a “raw endpoint”. These data will be collected prospectively, not retrospectively.

101. e - Kaplan Meier is a type of survival analysis.

102. a - This is a depiction of the probability of not having an event or endpoint. Think of it this way; as we age we our risk of not dying (i.e., living) decreases. It's the same way with studies. As the study moves forward in time, patients' risk for not dying or having a negative endpoint also decreases. Kaplan Meier may only test one variable (not several) at a time. Log rank tests are always used for Kaplan Meier curves to determine statistically significant differences between groups. Cox proportional hazards is not used for this purpose. Investigators are able to censor data with Kaplan Meier. Censoring would be needed for patients who died or had a negative outcome from a cause like a motor vehicle accident, which may be completely unrelated to their exposure or treatment.

103. e - Note that the Kaplan Meier curves are increasing over time. This is a depiction of the probability of having an event or endpoint. Think of it this way; as we age we our risk for death increases. It's the same way with studies. As the study moves forward in time, patients' risk for death or a negative outcome also increases.

104. Log-rank tests are always used to test for differences between Kaplan-Meier curves. So whenever you see that the authors used log rank tests in their statistics, they performed a Kaplan Meier analysis.

105. one - Log rank tests can test for differences in 1 variable at a time.

106. c - Since several studies are included, by process of elimination, this could only be a meta-analysis or systematic review.

107. e

108. b - Mantel Haenszel does not help determine heterogeneity, so does not help determine if a fixed or random effects model should be used. All of the others do.

109. c - Since p (0.7) is $\leq \alpha$ (0.1), heterogeneity is detected, so a random effects model like DerSimonian and Laird should be used for this MA.

110. b - Since p (0.07) is $\geq \alpha$ (0.05), heterogeneity is not detected, so a fixed effects model like Mantel Haenszel should be used for this MA.

111. d - Increasing sample size would increase power to detect a difference if one exists; this would decrease risk for type 2 error, not increase it. Different researchers have different abilities and relationships with other researchers. Some researchers may be have contacts that would allow them to include unpublished studies which are not known or accessible to other researchers. In this question, we are not provided enough information about the internal/external validity and types of studies included to know if it would be considered strong enough to be hypothesis proving.

112. a

113. b - This is publication bias against studies demonstrating neutrality. All of the included published studies show either benefit or detriment, but none of the included studies show neutrality. It is very likely that studies showing neutrality were refused for publication whereas studies showing either benefit or detriment were published.

114. e - All of the answers are possible reasons for only finding published studies showing benefit or no difference.

References

1. Gaddis & Gaddis: Introduction to Biostatistics; Part 1, Basic Concepts. *Annals of Emergency Medicine* 1990;19(1):86-89.
2. Gaddis & Gaddis: Introduction to Biostatistics; Part 2, Descriptive Statistics. *Annals of Emergency Medicine* 1990;19(3):309-315.
3. Gaddis & Gaddis: Introduction to Biostatistics; Part 3, Sensitivity, Specificity, Predictive Value, and Hypothesis Testing. *Annals of Emergency Medicine* 1990;19(5):591-597.
4. Gaddis & Gaddis: Introduction to Biostatistics; Part 4, Statistical Inference Techniques in Hypothesis Testing. *Annals of Emergency Medicine* 1990;19(7):820-825.
5. Gaddis & Gaddis: Introduction to Biostatistics; Part 5, Statistical Inference Techniques for Hypothesis Testing with Nonparametric Data. *Annals of Emergency Medicine* 1990;19(9):1054-1059.
    a. Adapted from Figure 4 Gaddis & Gaddis: Introduction to Biostatistics; Part 5, Statistical Inference Techniques for Hypothesis Testing with Nonparametric Data. *Annals of Emergency Medicine* 1990;19(9):1057 with permission from American College of Emergency Physicians.
    b. Adapted from Table Gaddis & Gaddis: Introduction to Biostatistics; Part 5, Statistical Inference Techniques for Hypothesis Testing with Nonparametric Data. *Annals of Emergency Medicine* 1990;19(9):1058 with permission from American College of Emergency Physicians.
6. Gaddis & Gaddis: Introduction to Biostatistics; Part 6, Correlation and Regression. *Annals of Emergency Medicine* 1990;19(12):1462-1468.
7. Glasner AN. *High Yield Biostatistics*. PA, Williams & Wilkins, 1995.
8. DeYoung GR. *Biostatistics: A Refresher* (handout). 2000 Updates in Therapeutics: The Pharmacotherapy Preparatory Course.
9. DeYoung GR. *Clinical Trial Design* (handout). 2000 Updates in Therapeutics: The Pharmacotherapy Preparatory Course.
10. DeYoung GR. *Biostatistical Applications* (handout). 2000 Updates in Therapeutics: The Pharmacotherapy Preparatory Course.
11. Kaye KS. *Clinical Epidemiology and Biostatistics: Overview and Basic Concepts* (handout). Faculty Development Seminar, Campbell University School of Pharmacy, Department of Pharmacy Practice, 2001.
12. Kaye KS. *Clinical Epidemiology and Biostatistics, Part 2* (handout). Faculty Development Seminar, Campbell University School of Pharmacy, Department of Pharmacy Practice, 2001.
13. Drew R. *Clinical Research Introduction* (handout). Drug Literature Evaluation/Applied Statistics Course. Campbell University School of Pharmacy, 2003.
14. Phelps K. *Statistical Calculations* (handout), 2001.
15. Berensen NM. *Statistics; A Review* (handout), 2001.
16. Discussions and provisions of Richard Drew, PharmD, MS, BCPS
17. Berensen NM. *Biostatistics review with lecture for the MUSC/VAMC BCPS study group*, Charleston, SC, July 17,2000.
18. Discussions with Antoine Al-Achi, PhD

19. Norman GR, Streiner,DL. *Biostatistics: The Bare Essentials, 2nd edition*. NY, B.C. Decker Inc. 2000.
20. Goyvaerts H. *Statistics for Non-Statisticians* (handout). Presentation for ABEMEP, May 22, 2002.
21. Salmi R, Desenclos JC, Moren A, Grein T. *Introduction to Logistic Regression*. www.epiet.org/.../ Introduction%20to%20logistic%20regression.ppt
22. ALLHAT - The Antihypertensive and Lipid-Lowering Treatment to Prevent Heart Attack Trial –3rd report – Major Cardiovascular Events in High-Risk Hypertensive Patients Randomized to ACEI or CCB or Diuretic. JAMA 2002;288(15):2981-2997.
23. ANBP2 - A Comparison of Outcomes with ACEIs and Diuretics for HTN in the Elderly. *NEJM.* 2003;348;7:583-92.
24. LIFE - Cardiovascular morbidity and mortality in the Losartan Intervention For Endpoint reduction in hypertension study: a randomized trial against atenolol. *Lancet.*2002;359:995-1003.
25. ValHeFT – A Randomized Trial of the Angiotensin-receptor blocker Valsartan in Chronic Heart Failure. *NEJM.* 2001;345(23);1667-75.
26. Cochrane online reviewer's handbook 4.2.0 http://www.cochrane.dk/cochrane/handbook/hbookHeterogeneity.htm
27. DeYoung GR. Understanding Statistics: An Approach for the Clinician. Science and Practice of Pharmacotherapy 1. PSAP Book 5, 5th ed., American College of Clinical Pharmacy, 2005.
28. Chart from reference 27 which was adapted with permission from the American College of Physicians-American Society of Internal Medicine. Froehlich GW. What is the chance that this study is clinically significant? A proposal for Q values. Eff Clin Pract 1999;2:234-9.
29. West PM. Literature Evaluation. Science and Practice of Pharmacotherapy 2. PSAP Book 5, 5th ed., American College of Clinical Pharmacy, 2005.
30. Snapinn SM. Commentary: Non-inferiority Trials. *Curr Control Trials Cardiovasc Med.* 2000; 1:19-21
31. The Cochrane Collaboration. Module 3: An introduction to meta-analysis http://www.cochrane-net.org/openlearning/HTML/mod3.htm
32. De Muth JE. *Basic Statistics and Pharmaceutical Statistical Applications, 2nd edition*. Boca Raton, London, New York, Chapman & Hall/CRC, Taylor & Francis Group. 2006.
33. Kelly WD, Ratliff, TA, Nenadic, C. *Basic Statistics for Laboratories*. John Wiley and Sons, Hoboken, NJ, 1992, p93.
34. Piaggio G, Elbourne DR, Altman DG, et al. Reporting of Non-inferiority and Equivalence Randomized Trials: An Extension of the CONSORT Statement. *JAMA.* 2006;295(10):1152-60.
35. Katz MH. Multivariable Analysis: A Primer for Readers of Medical Research. *Ann Intern Med.* 2003;138:644-50.
36. Strassels SA, Wilson JP. Pharmacoepidemiology. Science and Practice of Pharmacotherapy. PSAP Book 4, 6th ed., American College of Clinical Pharmacy, 2007.
37. Yang Yi, West-Strum D. *Understanding Pharmacoepidemiology*. McGraw Hill Medical, NY, 2011.

38. Foster, EM. Propensity Score Matching. *Medical Care.* 2003;41(10):1183-92.
39. Chen G, Wang YC, Chi GYH. Hypothesis and Type 1 Error in Active-Control Noninferiority Trials. *J of Biopharmaceutical Statistics*. 2004;14(2):301-13.
40. Christensen E. Methodology of superiority vs. equivalence trials and non-inferiority trials. *J Hepatology*. 2007; 46:947-54.
41. *Gehlbach SH Interpreting the Medical Literature, 4th edition, pg 181.*
42. Shargel L, Wu-Pong S, Yu A. *Applied Biopharmaceutics & Pharmacokinetics*, 6th ed. New York, NY: McGraw-Hill; 2012.
43. General methods for Cochrane reviews; part 2, chapter 9, section 9.5 (heterogeneity) http://handbook.cochrane.org/chapter_9/9_5_2_identifying_and_measuring_heterogeneity.htm - accessed June 2014.
44. Aparasu RR, Bentley J. *Principles of Research Design and Drug Literature Evaluation*. Burlington, MA: Jones and Bartlett Learning; 2015.
45. Kernan WN, Viscoli CM, Makuch RW, et al. Stratified Randomization for Clinical Trials. *J Clin Epidemiol*. 52(1):19-26, 1999.

Index